JOURNEY

JOURNEY

A Spiritual Odyssey

PETER FRANCE

Chatto & Windus
LONDON

Published by Chatto & Windus 1998

2 4 6 8 10 9 7 5 3 1

Copyright © Peter France 1998

First published in 1998 by Chatto & Windus
Random House, 20 Vauxhall Bridge Road, London SW1V 2SA

Random House Australia (Pty) Limited
20 Alfred Street, Milsons Point, Sydney,
New South Wales, 2061, Australia

Random House New Zealand Limited
18 Poland Road, Glenfield,
Auckland 10, New Zealand

Random House South Africa (Pty) Limited
Endulini, 5A Jubilee Road, Parktown 2193, South Africa

Random House UK Limited Reg. No. 954009

A CIP catalogue record for this book
is available from the British Library

ISBN 0 7011 6696 7

Typeset by Deltatype Limited, Birkenhead, Merseyside

Printed and bound in Great Britain by
Mackays of Chatham PLC

To Felicia
who,
having watched me spend so much time
and energy
in scaling the battlements,
quietly
found the front door
and opened it

Acknowledgements

The idea that my journey might be of interest was put to me by Norman Stone who has to accept ultimate responsibility for this book, though not, of course, for its shortcomings. I hope he will also accept my gratitude.

In the process of writing, on Patmos, I was supported and stimulated by the prodigious memory and library of my friend Carraigh B. Thomson, who never hesitated to make both available to me.

In trying to find words to express the change of conviction in the final chapters, I was inspired by the writings of the great Russian philosopher, S.L. Frank. I shall always be indebted to him for his insights and to his grandson, Peter Scorer, for making them available to me.

Finally, a book which records changes in perspective over sixty years owes everything to the people who brought them about. They are too numerous to mention, even to remember, since what they gave to me has become part of myself. I am always grateful.

Contents

Chapter One

Father Christmas was not a Wise Man. You could see from his shape that he spent more hours at his table than at his telescope, and his face had the open, cheerful expression of somebody who doesn't waste a lot of time thinking. He was a dumpy figure in a short red tunic with a hood; the Magi were tall, gaunt and serious, with striped turbans and long sepia robes. But Father Christmas stood with them on a brass tray in front of the chapel pulpit; and he looked, with them, at the baby wrapped in strips of cloth and lying on a handful of hay. I think there were shepherds as well. I remember a few sheep. And definitely cattle, whose lowing, we sang, woke the baby.

Christmas in the village of Clifton, near Brighouse, Yorkshire, when I was a small boy, was a time of wonder. It was the season for the suspension of disbelief. Just for a few days, once a year, the village would unite in a benign conspiracy to celebrate fantasy. As children, we were its focus. The world of fantasy was our territory, and we were a bit surprised when the grown-ups came to join us there once a year. We always forgot that they would go back to their own world when the season was over.

At the age of around eight or nine, some of us colluded with them in keeping secret the identity of the man behind the false white whiskers at the Co-op. But I could never quite get a straight answer about the shepherds and the wise men who stood with Father Christmas on the brass tray in the chapel. I did notice that quite a lot of the people who joined us on the village green before Christmas and sang enthusiastically about shepherds watching their flocks by night, or three kings of Orient following yonder star, didn't show up at chapel for the rest of the year. And it didn't take long to work out that they too were part of the conspiracy. Father Christmas with his reindeer, shepherds with their little lambs, wise men and their gifts – all these were part of the fantasy world the grown-ups came together to pretend to believe in once a year for the sake of the kids. But what about the Little Lord Jesus asleep on the hay?

Well, at Sunday school we sang that there's a friend for little children above the bright blue sky, and that Jesus wants me for a sunbeam to shine for him each day. We couldn't imagine that he would pick out as a sunbeam middle-aged spinsters like Nelly Ramsbottom or Violet Nobbs, or even the local squire, Sir George Armytage. So any shining that was called for would have to be done by us kids. Jesus, too, along with the other figures on the brass tray, was strictly for the children.

But there was a problem here: quite a few of the grown-ups went on singing about Jesus all the year round, as if he were somehow different. As if they even believed that he really had existed. Some of them even spoke as if he still did exist, that we had such a friend in Jesus – all our pains and griefs to bear. But I couldn't help noticing that they weren't the cleverest or most successful people in the village. Perhaps Jesus was only a reality for the failures, the people who needed his help. I noticed that these people seemed to be the ones with the most pain and grief to bear. Their faces were tight and drawn as they sat on the chapel benches in uncomfortable clothes. There was no laughter in chapel. It seemed to me that these people were trying so very hard to be good; and being good took such a lot out of them.

I also decided that they must be not very intelligent. I had read somewhere that intelligence is the ability to learn from experience. These people would pray every Sunday for something that didn't happen: they would ask for the recovery of sick people, who then died; they would pray to God to help and protect our troops in battle, and they lost; they would ask in summer for seasonable weather, and it poured.

I don't remember, as a child, having a great problem with unanswered prayer. Jesus had told us that if we really believed that he could move a mountain, and we asked him, he would do it. But I knew that I could never convince myself that he could. I did try, just once. We didn't have any mountains around Clifton, but there were the 'pit hills' – slag heaps overgrown with grass where we used to play. And I once knelt in the grass and closed my eyes and asked him to slide them a couple of yards nearer to the fence to prove to me that he meant what he said. But when I opened my eyes again the pit hills had stayed where they were. Just as I expected. And I had to admit to myself that I never really believed they would move. So I accepted that my prayers would never be answered because I could never truly believe. And I supposed that applied to everybody who prayed.

I was sent to Sunday school to get me out of the house. I remember reading some social historian who revealed that the only way working-class couples could reproduce themselves in their cramped and overcrowded dwellings was by sending the kids off to Sunday school so they had a brief time on their own. There were five of us – four boys and a girl – and I was the middle one. We all had a taste of Sunday school.

My dad was not a religious man. He was born in 1900 – a bad time to arrive if you wanted to hold fast to the idea of a loving God and a Christian society. At eighteen he was driving a team of mules through the mud of the battlefields of France; in his early thirties he was stuck in the recession and handing out bread and dripping to the Jarrow marchers. He was getting properly on his feet and looking forward to a peaceful and prosperous future only by 1939.

Dad had little formal education. He had been taught at the

village school by Mr Tomlinson, himself not a scholar but a long-distance runner who had done a crash course to become a teacher when the laws on compulsory education were changed and there was a national shortage of teachers. Dad left school at twelve years old and got a job, first as an 'oiler and takker off' in a cotton mill at Brighouse and then, following the family tradition, at Hartshead pit. His job as a fourteen-year-old was to sort the coal 'on t'shakker', which meant standing by a conveyor belt and picking out the shale and stones from the pieces of coal as they passed along. His ambition was to work with his dad down the pit as a 'ripper': to crouch up against the coalface and hack away at the seam with a short-handled pick. It helped to be compact if you were a 'ripper'. Short arms and legs with a broad chest. The France genes had supplied these.

But it was not to be. The pit manager was keen to have another France down the mine but grandad objected. There was a row in the manager's office. 'The day I see *thy* son working at t'coal face,' said grandad to the boss, 'I'll let my lad down to work alongside 'im.' So they were both given their cards and sent down the fields back home. Dad got a job apprenticed to a butcher, a trade he then followed for the rest of his life. He rented a smallholding from Sir George Armytage; on this he planted potatoes, grazed a house cow and brought up five children. He had been promoted, though he never realized it to the end of his days, in the eyes of the Registrar General from the working-class to the lower middle.

Dad would never have accepted the classification. To be working-class was a matter of social loyalty, not of employment. He called himself working-class all his life, and had the clearest vision of the eternal conflict of class interests. Quite simply, what was good for the bosses was bad for the workers: the one fought for longer hours and shorter wages; the other for the opposite. And this basic conflict was reflected in life as a whole. There were men with soft hands and posh voices who had to be treated with respect if they had power over us. But their interests were not ours. Things which operated to their benefit were on that account harmful to us, no matter how they tried to conceal this. To be unaware of this – to vote Tory, for example – was to show stupidity. To join the soft-handed was to be a class traitor.

He never discussed religion with us, but I know he had a passion for the truth and felt that Christianity was unaccept-able because parsons told lies in the interest of maintaining the inequalities of a social system in which they had a comfortable place. His attachment to truth was so strong that he hated baby talk. A horse was a horse and not a gee-gee. It was wrong to corrupt a child's mind with untruth, so the books he bought us were encyclopaedias and not fairy tales.

He felt the chapel was for the working-class and the church for the others. And he criticized both – as did, and do, outsiders – for being hypocritical: for claiming virtues they didn't practise. He followed Marxist economic doctrine in accepting that the basic injustice in society was caused by the bosses misappropriating the economic surplus to their bene-fit. So he probably also accepted Marx's idea that the bosses fed religion to the people like opium to keep them quiet. The only comment of his I can remember on the subject was that it seemed strange, when Christians claimed we were all equal in the sight of God, that they should reserve in church a special pew for Sir George Armytage in which other members of the congregation were not allowed to pray.

Whatever distaste he felt for religion, it didn't stop him sending us off to Sunday school every week. At the Methodist chapel we were part of the institution that had been the seedbed of the Labour Party. The text painted on the wall read BLESSED ARE THE MEEK FOR THEY SHALL INHERIT THE EARTH. And we were taught that Jesus loved the poor. Our life on earth, we learned, is harsh; but if we go short in this life we shall rejoice in the next. We took no small pleasure from the reassurance that the well-to-do were in for a hard time. Our favourite biblical text was the

Magnificat: 'He hath filled the hungry with good things; *and the rich he hath sent empty away.*'

We felt a bit smug about the middle-classes who went to the Church of England across the road, and I enjoyed picturing them in the afterlife as a crowd of camels bumping against the needle's eye. Chapel made us secure on the bottom rung. The preacher, Dad pointed out, had muck under his fingernails. He knew about real life. He had worked for a living.

I was taken to Clifton Chapel before I could walk, by a devout spinster called Ada Hopper. Ada was a living demonstration of the principle that the strength of belief in the goodness of God is in inverse proportion to the evidence. She was always poor. Her father had died when she was a child – on Christmas Eve. Her betrothed was killed in the First World War, and she decided to give her life to Jesus. She worked every day in the dust and grime and among the clattering machinery of a cotton mill; she spent her evenings reading the Bible or teaching it to children. She loved children.

Ada had what we called in the village 'religious mania'. By that we meant that she tried to live her life like a disciple of Jesus, in humility and with love for everybody. She would not have been out of place in an enclosed religious order. In the industrial North she seemed simple-minded. You couldn't cope with real life without craft and the assertion of self-interest. These were the qualities we admired. The so-called 'Christian' virtues of self-sacrifice, humility and love for your neighbour – and even more incredibly for your enemy – were fine for the parsons who didn't have to work for a living. The rest of us could not afford them.

For some reason, Ada had a particular affection for me. It could have been because, as a small boy, I looked particularly angelic, with blue eyes and a bubbly mass of light-yellow curly hair. Appearances in small boys can be especially deceptive. She would pick me up from home and take me to the chapel, where I sat on the back steps and crushed the stems of daffodils as she arranged the flowers for the glory of God and told me if I would only take Jesus into my heart it would be filled with joy. The word 'joy' she would whisper close to my face, drawing back her lips from her teeth with her eyes shining earnestly. She spoke the word with an ardour that approached ferocity, and I was embarrassed. Whatever 'joy' meant to her, I could see there was little comfort in it and no pleasure. I shrank away from the invitation: my sights were set on getting as much as I could of both.

So I crossed the road to the Anglican church where the environment was plusher. Members of the congregation there lived in clean stone semis instead of soot-stained back-to-back cottages. They had pianos in the front room and antimacassars on the armchairs. Their newspapers were (I knew because I did the paper round) the *Daily Mail* and the *Daily Express*. One even took *The Times*. Not a *Daily Herald* or a *Daily Worker* among them. And I knew this meant they were content with their lot and keen to preserve it against the ambitions of the less fortunate. The vicar's name was painted in gold letters on a black noticeboard outside the church followed by '(M.A. Oxon)'. I remember my dad once pointing to this and cautioning, 'That shows he's not one of us.' But the vicar lived in a big house with sweeping lawns; he spoke like a BBC announcer; he had soft white hands; he had plenty of money and had clearly never done a day's work in his life. He was a man I could learn things from.

There was another attraction. In the porch of the church hung a notice listing all the archbishops of Canterbury since the foundation of the see by St Augustine, via Taetwine, Breogwine and Joenbehrt right down to Cosmo Gordon Lang, who held the position when I joined his Church in 1941. It claimed that St Augustine was in direct line from the Apostles, and so Cosmo Gordon Lang was too – an impressive historical connection. This had to be the real thing.

The final draw was the promise of cash – for the first time

in my life I discovered that it was possible to earn money without getting physically tired. On offer at the Church of St John was sixpence a week for boys who sang in the choir. The money was written against your name every Sunday so long as you had turned up for Friday choir practice and put in your stint at matins and evensong. But there was a shrewd condition attached to the pay-out: choirboys would receive their accumulated sixpences only if they stayed with the choir until their voices broke. By the time this happened, of course, adolescence had struck and boys had better things to do with their Friday evenings than attend choir practice. As I remember, nobody ever stayed on to collect the cash.

The question of confirmation came up. I had decided that no sane and intelligent person would ever consent to be confirmed, because so long as you could dodge the ceremony you were not responsible to God for your behaviour: all your sins fell on your godparents. Out of a cautious self-interest and under threat from the recording angel, I had already begun a tentative reading of theology and I discovered that my godparents had, at baptism, promised that I would 'renounce the devil and all his works, the vain pomp and glory of the world, with all covetous desires of the same and the carnal desires of the flesh'. They had done this on my behalf when I was in no position to speak for myself. *I* had made no such promise. To be confirmed was to take over the responsibility for an undertaking which, even in my pre-adolescent years, I sensed might be foolhardy.

How I was expected, at the age of ten, to have come to the conclusion that a being called God had made me and the world, with not a jot of evidence for either supposition, I found hard to understand. Yet, if I consented to be confirmed, I had to declare my belief in this before a bishop and witnesses, and undertake that I would not allow my manservant nor my maidservant nor my cattle nor the stranger that is within my gates to do any manner of work on Sundays. There was plenty to talk about. I decided that intellectual honesty forced me to delay acceptance of confirmation until I could be convinced that affirmations I was expected to make in public were true. In the meantime the recording angel would have to stay his pencil or write up my misdeeds in somebody else's ledger.

In 1942, when I was eleven, I passed 'for the grammar'. That is, I had managed enough marks in a county minor scholarship to be allotted a place at Rastrick Grammar School, a seventeenth-century foundation in a village four miles away with an enrolment of 150 boys and a staff of twelve teachers. This meant that I travelled on the morning bus at 8.22 each day, wearing a red and black cap which I had persuaded my eldest brother to run over several times on his motor bike so it would not look new. I always tried for the seat three up from the back, because it sat over the axle and alongside the wheelbox. So it was a single seat. I could read undisturbed.

I really can't remember how much of my reading at the time was slaking a thirst for knowledge and how much was a pose. I had heard friends of the family telling my mother that they thought my brain would be turned soft if she wasn't careful because 'he always has his nose in a book'. Because I had a habit of cleaning my teeth, which was thought to be an unmanly concern with personal appearance, they already suspected that I might be developing into a homosexual. Families often create roles for the children to act out. There were five of us, and from the age of about ten I was 'the Prof': a bit soft in the head, never knows what day it is, forgetful, 'would lose his head if it were loiss [not fixed on]'. So I acted out the role and would never appear in public without a book. When I did the shopping at the local Co-op, about quarter of a mile away, I would walk there and back with a shopping basket in one hand and a book in the other. And I wouldn't raise my eyes from the page except to fill the basket at the shop and empty it at home.

Much of what I read at the time I couldn't understand. I followed two rules in the choice of book: (1) it must be 'true', that is, factual – I could not abide fiction, since there was no point in cramming a developing brain with lies – and (2) it must be adult, since children's books were for children and I was at grammar school. The rich world of the child's imagination was closed to me. I wanted to know things which were so, and had no concern with things which were not.

I was for a time mildly frustrated at not looking like a professor. Professors were tall and gaunt from much studying and always had thick glasses. I was rather short and thick-set, and my eyesight was fine. I was intimidated, I remember, by boys with glasses at the grammar school, because I thought that they must have read a great deal more than I. But when the examination results placed bespectacled scholars below me, I grew in self-confidence.

About this time I discovered the classical Greeks. They were, I understood, clever and had laid the foundations of intellectual life in Europe. But they were also physically fit. They took a pride in their bodies. They even had muscles which showed. And it occurred to me that, if I couldn't aspire to the wilting physique of the intellectuals I admired – Bertrand Russell, Aldous Huxley, Bernard Shaw – then I would try to be a classical Greek and cultivate a sane mind in a healthy body. I read the account of Milon, the most famous wrestler at the Olympic games, who built up his strength by lifting a newborn calf on to his shoulders and then picking up the animal each day as it grew until he was able to march around the Olympic stadium with a fully grown bull on his shoulders. He then killed it and ate it in a single day. I did not believe the last bit of the story, but I had no weight-training equipment and my dad had started to rear calves so I picked up one of them one morning and tried to sling it across my shoulders. It kicked me in the eye and made a mess down my shirt, so my mother told me not to try again.

Then I discovered, from the magazine *Health and Strength*, that there was a weightlifting club in a pub called the Rising Sun at Scholes, about three miles away. I began training three times a week, pedalling furiously there and back on my bike to strengthen heart and lungs, and working seriously through a programme of exercises to reduce or enlarge different bits of me so that I would end up physically perfect. There were at the time two different schools of thought in the body-building world. One, led by the Americans, believed that more is better and concentrated on building bigger bodies, so that the winners of their competitions were the ones who clocked up most inches on the tape-measure. The other school, led by the French, taught that we should aim at balance and proportion: twice round the wrist is once round the neck; twice round the neck is once round the waist; and so on. They published the vital statistics of Greek statues, and urged us to imitate them. I attached myself to the French school.

It was while bicycling to and from the Rising Sun that twin ambitions formed in my mind. I wanted above all things to be clever and I was excited at the prospect of looking like a Greek god, so I decided to aim at being appointed a fellow of All Souls College, Oxford, and winning the Mr Universe contest in the same year. In furtherance of the first ambition I decided to commit to memory the contents of the *Everyman Encyclopaedia*, which we had in the school library. I looked at the spines every morning: A to BAD; BAD to BRI; BRI to CHU; CHU to DEN; DEN to FIL etc. I was a fast reader and had a good memory, so could see no reason why, in the course of my five years at Rastrick Grammar School, I should not learn the lot and then nobody could deny me a scholarship to Oxford and the rest was easy. I was reasonably certain that the three sessions a week pumping iron over the public bar of the Rising Sun would make me swell in all the right places. Life seemed set fair for a career as an intellectual Adonis.

The first doubts struck when I reached the Bayeux Tapestry, which had a crisp entry in Volume 2 of the *Everyman*. To astonish any future examiner, I had tucked away in the back of my brain the fact that it is 231 feet long and 20 inches wide when I realized I no longer knew who

Aaron's wife was nor whether the aardvark was confined to
Africa or India. I could read at great speed, I could hold in
my brain a large number of facts; but the understanding
dawned that they didn't hang around in there. This was a
revelation. I had never thought that if I once knew something
I could cease to know it just through the passage of time. All
Souls began to recede.

The body seemed to be swelling satisfactorily towards
perfection. I had sent away to *Health and Strength* my vital
statistics, including wrist and ankle size, height and weight,
with a full-frontal snap of me in bathing trunks with my belly
sucked in so they could tell whether I was an endomorph
(wide chest, long abdomen, short legs) or an ectomorph (long
chest, short abdomen, long legs). In return I had received a
chart telling me the various measurements I should aim at on
my way to becoming Mr Universe. My weekly sessions with
the tape-measure were encouraging, and I was having serious
thoughts about competing for the junior Mr Yorkshire
contest, or perhaps junior Mr West Riding of Yorkshire,
when I was called to the headmaster's office one morning. It
had come to his attention that I was spending my evenings at
a public house. Worse, that I was taking off my clothes and
striding about half-naked in a room over the public bar. Did I
really think this behaviour gentlemanly? I had no idea at the
time of how gentlemen behaved, but supposed that I should
be making some attempts to find out. The headmaster said
something about the honour of the school and his duty to
shape character as well as train minds and let his disapproval
of the Rising Sun Weight Lifting and Body Building Club
hang in the air without being shaped into specific words. It
was enough. I gave up thoughts of rippling my well-oiled
muscles on a spotlit podium and spent more time on my
homework.

Religion was not on the curriculum and I had no time for
it, since all the hours I had were given to subjects that would
be examined. Religious writings seemed to me to be enter-
tainments, like novels, indulging in fantasies – relaxations for

those with time to spare. I had none. I was specially keen on the sciences: chemistry, physics, biology and mathematics – all pandering to the lust for certainty, for understanding the world as it was, rather than as some people imagined it to be. I was particularly keen on nuclear physics, which it seemed to me was the one discipline that dealt with ultimate reality. As we sat down at the kitchen table, there was something thrilling about realizing that the table wasn't really made of solid wood but of billions of tiny atoms, each with a positively charged nucleus round which were spinning negatively charged electrons like microscopic billiard balls. And I was the only person sitting at the table to know this. More than anything else I wanted to be a scientist, a nuclear physicist, so that I could come to understand the ultimates.

Every Sunday I sang in the church choir. I saw people 'being religious'. They stood up and confessed to each other and to their God that they were miserable sinners and that there was no health in them but nobody really believed it – least of all themselves. Most incomprehensibly of all, to me, they kept singing praises to God as if he was in constant need of the reassurance of being told how wonderful he was.

As a member of the choir I took part in these ceremonies, comforting myself with the thought that I was only in it for the money and that, if the sentiments expressed were cant, the music was often beautiful. But there was one moment in the service when I could not distance myself from what was going on: the recital of the Creed. Everyone stood and spoke aloud the words 'I believe in one God, the Father Almighty, Maker of heaven and earth . . .' Now I did not believe any such thing. So how could I, with integrity, stand up in public and say that I did? I thought a good deal about it, and worked out that if God did not exist, there could be no harm at all in getting to my feet and saying I believed that he did; if, on the other hand, if he were around somewhere, he would know that I was lying when I did it. So every week I stood and mouthed the words with my fingers crossed behind my back. Just in case.

The general attitude of the Church of England, as represented in the village of Clifton, was that people who attended Sunday services were giving public witness to their acceptance of middle-class standards of dress and behaviour. We had not yet reached the stage when bishops could go public with denials of the basic traditional Christian beliefs; but it would not do to inquire too closely into how many of the supernatural claims of the Church were accepted by members of the congregation. When I questioned the ones I knew well enough to approach, the answers I got were guarded and, I felt, rather tense – as if I had asked them about their sex lives. I sensed that if religion, like sex, was something for grown-ups to be embarrassed about and hidden, it was probably, like sex, worth investigating.

This meant simply reading the right books. By this time in life I had decided that anything could be learned from books. People, I discovered, spent their lives acquiring expertise, and then some of them wrote it all down. So I could pick up and make my own, in a couple of hours, knowledge that had been gradually brought together over forty years. Somebody had written a book about every subject under the sun. If I needed to know how to build a drystone wall or plant vegetables or tune a carburettor, I would find the answer in a book, just as I could find out the structure of the French language, the gross national product of Peru or the proof of the theorem of Pythagoras.

When it came to religion, I discovered there were two classes of book to be examined. The first, by committed religious people, didn't take long to discard, because they were all starting from a point I hadn't reached. That is, they were accepting propositions the truth of which I was seeking to establish. The second class, by philosophers who were using their intellectual powers to discover truth, was much more attractive. I also decided when I passed for the grammar that, since the word 'philosopher' meant a lover of knowledge, then I must be one. A person can be a lover of knowledge without having acquired very much.

The first contact I made with the world's great philosophers was disappointing. I read a survey of great thinkers
from Plato to the present day in one of the many compendi-
ums of knowledge in the local public library. Most of them
seemed to be putting their energies into proving the obvious
or arguing about formulas of words to express something
everybody knew to be true. I could understand only a few of
the arguments and was becoming disillusioned with philosophy when Mr Baldwin set me right.

Mr Baldwin was the village communist. He lived in a small
terraced house with an interior unusual in the community
because it contained books and because they were housed in
beautifully carved shelving. Mr Baldwin had been a wood-
carver by profession. He intrigued me because he had earned
his living making beautiful objects for use in churches –
ornate lecterns, scrolled pulpits, pew ends with networks of
birds, oak leaves and acorns – and yet he did not believe in
God. More than that: he was a settled and totally convinced
atheist. I longed to ask him how he managed to reconcile the
advancement of the cause of atheism with the beautification
of churches, but he was not a communicative man. At least,
he did not say much to an inquisitive boy. He did lend me
books published in the Soviet Union, from which I gathered
that the beauties of the churches there were thought of as
part of the cultural heritage of the country, to be preserved
and enjoyed even in the modern age when Christianity had
been exposed as exploitation. I decided that this must be his
justification for his work.

Mr Baldwin had a lot of time for Jesus Christ. He told me
that Jesus was the world's first true communist – hating the
rich, loving the poor, and preaching a gospel of share and
share alike. The first disciples, as reported in the Acts of the
Apostles, had put his teaching into action by creating the first
organized cells of communism, where hundreds of people
had lived together, selling all their goods and giving the
money to their society, and owning everything in common.
Of course the forces of reaction and privilege had taken over

and turned Christ's message from a social to a spiritual one so that they could continue to tolerate and eventually to preach inequality in his name. All of this I accepted as the obvious truth, and I developed a strong respect for Mr Baldwin's wisdom, so that when he told me one day that if I was looking for a philosopher then Marcus Aurelius was my man, I went straight for Marcus Aurelius.

The first chapter of *The Golden Book* convinced me that this was a philosopher to listen to. In it, the Roman Emperor – the most powerful man in the world of his day – thanks his mother for having taught him to live frugally on a spare diet and his father for never caring about the clothes he wore. Clothes were always a problem to me, not just because I had no money to buy them but because even if I had had the money I should not have known how to spend it. Out of uniform I always felt that what I had on was more or less inappropriate to the situation I was in. This feeling has only recently begun to recede. Marcus Aurelius told me it did not matter, and I believed him.

I also believed him when he wrote about the importance of living an independent life: 'To be cheerful, and stand in no need, either of other men's help or attendance or of that rest and tranquillity which thou must be beholding to others for.' I took this as a golden rule throughout my teenage years. As a natural loner, I delighted in the discovery of an authentication of unsociability. Clearly the philosophical rules I adopted were not shaping my character; I was just selecting the ones which confirmed my prejudices.

I remember copying with delight the words of Marcus Aurelius which illustrate how we should see through and so properly assess things which society tends to overvalue. In the quaint seventeenth-century translation by Meric Casaubon printed in the *Everyman* edition they read, 'This purple robe is but sheep's hairs dyed with the blood of a shell-fish. So for coitus, it is but the attrition of an ordinary base entrail, and the excretion of a little vile snivel, with a certain kind of convulsion.' There is nothing quite so reassuring as being told that what is missing from your life is trivial.

Another aspect of the stoic philosophy which I found reassuring was the attitude to death. For Marcus Aurelius, 'Death is a cessation from the impression of the senses, the tyranny of the passions, the errors of the mind and the servitude of the body.' During the years I spent in the throes of adolescence, I was from time to time obsessed with death, as is quite normal for the condition, and I was glad to be able to accept it on these terms. Further, since death is inevitable, Marcus Aurelius points out that it is ridiculous to be upset or resentful if it arrives one day rather than the next. And, if life should become too hard to bear, then the sensible course of action is to help oneself out of it. This was the honourable way, the Roman way, the course chosen by Mark Antony and reported with such poetry and dignity by Shakespeare (*Antony and Cleopatra* was one of our set books). It was obvious that the taboos against helping oneself to shuffle off were cultural and local, since neither the Romans nor the Japanese had them, so I decided after Marcus Aurelius that life need never be unbearably painful. After that, life seemed far more enjoyable and secure.

It was on my paper round one day that a seed was planted that was to change my life. I always ran round the village delivering the papers, partly because I thought the exercise would increase my chest girth and also because, incredibly as it seems at this distance in time, running was actually easier than walking. It seemed more natural and took no self-control. On this day, I was dashing along a row of terraced cottages when I heard a sound from one of them that took my breath away. There were waves caressing the sands, the swish of waving palm trees, liquid voices singing in simple harmonies a language that seemed all vowels, accompanied by the sensuous swooning of an electric guitar. I had never before heard Hawaiian music; its impact was immediate, physical and entrancing. I stood until the record came to an end, and walked for the rest of the paper round in a daze.

After that experience I used to stand and listen outside the cottage whenever the music sounded. One day the door opened and the owner asked me in. His name was Wilfred Smith. He was fascinated by the South Seas, and had a collection of records of music from Hawaii, Samoa, Tahiti and the exotic islands that, during the war years, had a special attraction for the pinched communities in Britain squeezed by rationing and the blackout. Some of the music was from dance bands that aped a fancied Pacific island idiom because it was popular: A. P. Sharpe and His Honolulu Hawaiians; Felix Mendelson and his Hawaiian Serenaders. Then there were the ones closer to the authentic: Sol Hoopi and his Novelty Five. Wilfred Smith taught me to pick out the 'real stuff' from the imitation and helped me learn the words to 'Makala pua' and 'Ke kali nei au', which I did not understand but chanted to myself as I ran along the village.

This was the first, seemingly intimate because directly experienced, contact with an exotic culture. Not everybody, I was learning, thought and lived as we did in Clifton. There were sun-soaked islands far away where you tickled the earth and it laughed back a harvest; where the lagoons were loaded with fish; where girls with skin the colour of milk chocolate played ukeleles, red hibiscuses in their hair and garlands of heavy-scented frangipani nestling over their naked breasts. Well, I think those were the images that came to mind as I heard and sang the songs of the South Seas. And I decided that one day I would go there. It was a form of escapism very popular during the war years.

My other form of escapism was the theatre. The first time I appeared on stage was in the leading role of *The Emperor's New Clothes* at Clifton Primary School. The part gave me more anxiety than any I have played since then; I spent weeks of sleepless nights after being cast in it. As the opening night approached I seriously considered running away from home or even falling, like Mark Antony, on my sword. This had nothing to do with diffidence or lack of self-confidence in my acting abilities. It had everything to do with underpants, of which I had never heard.

The Emperor, you remember, spends much of his time in his shirt and nothing else, because the tailor has sold him clothes that can be seen only by the pure in heart. Now this meant that I was expected to walk about on the stage of the village school, in front of an audience of parents and, worse still, elder sisters, wearing a shirt and nothing else. Who knew what a gust from the wings or even too brisk a turn might reveal? I daren't, of course, discuss my terrors with the teacher in charge, and they were dissipated only when she asked me, just before the dress rehearsal, what sort of bathing trunks I would be wearing under the shirt. I felt as Androcles must have felt when the lion licked his hand. Life was suddenly golden again, and I played with aplomb.

Acting became important quite soon after that. I discovered that I was good at it. I played Shakespeare at grammar school and with the Brighouse Children's Theatre. We toured the Yorkshire Dales with productions of *Twelfth Night* and *The Merchant of Venice* in which I played the roles of Toby Belch and Shylock. The local papers gave us good reviews and the mayor and corporation a civic reception, so we must have made a good impression.

Acting was important to me because it was the only thing I could do in which I felt complete self-confidence. Off-stage, meeting people in ordinary social situations generated in me only different levels of mortification. I was always conscious of being the working-class lad from Clifton. True, I had passed for the grammar; I was even doing rather well there: I had read lots of books and was familiar with the causes of the First World War, French irregular verbs and the disposition of the planets in the solar system. But I couldn't choose a tie or address an envelope. And the odd thing is that, in the English social system, there seems to be an assumption that manners, etiquette, patterns of behaviour are innate. They are programmed into your genes or you absorb them with your mother's milk. They are a matter of breeding, of instinct rather than learning. So nobody can be ignorant of them. This creates a problem which I became aware of when I was very young. I discovered that nobody minded if I told them I didn't know anything that could be taught – I could confess to anyone that I had not yet learned the rules of grammar, even the rules of cricket – but ignorance of the rules of behaviour was morally culpable. People were shocked by it. I was ignorant but could not admit it, so I tried to avoid social situations because I always felt insecure in them.

But on stage I knew the rules. The language, gestures, movements were given by somebody else, and once I had them by heart I could put them over with assurance. It isn't difficult to impress an audience with your verbal fluency when the words you are using were put in your mouth by Shakespeare. I don't quite know where the assurance came from, but I can never remember a time when I did not feel, however unjustifiably, a complete self-confidence on stage which I could not approach off it until my late fifties.

The greatest pleasure in playing Shakespeare is simply speaking beautiful words. I think this must be specially liberating in the north of England, where verbal fluency is suspect. 'Don't listen to what he says, watch what he does' is the basic rule for assessing our fellow men. The man of few words is admired, and the golden rule for all Yorkshiremen is 'Hear all, see all, say nowt.' So words are not admired, and the ability to speak, being thought the least significant of the evolutionary developments that distinguish humanity from the rest of the animal kingdom, is rarely and grudgingly exercised. The Yorkshire dialect is guttural, as if the words are kept back in the throat and let out reluctantly, as opposed to the palatal, tip-of-the-tongue chattering of the South. So poetry was for me a release. I read furiously and uncritically. A side effect of this was that I began to get better marks in English than in any other subject, and so, although I still hankered after the sciences, I decided to transfer to the arts so that I should be doing what I seemed best at.

I still have a copy of a book called *The Heritage of Poetry*, chosen and edited by Philip Wayne and published during the war years on the slightly off-white cheap paper which was in use then. Inside the cover is a bookplate recording that I was awarded this volume in July 1946 as the Form IVa prize in English, which is not at all noteworthy since we were a small school and most people seemed to get prizes. What is revelatory and, to me, scarcely credible is that there are two pencilled page references under the plate to poems which I found particularly striking when I first read the book. The first is by Thomas Campion, and it reads:

> The man of life upright,
>   Whose guiltless heart is free
> From all dishonest deeds,
>   Or thought of vanity:
>
> The man whose silent days
>   In harmless joys are spent,
> Whom hopes cannot delude,
>   Nor sorrow discontent:
>
> That man needs neither towers
>   Nor armour for defence,
> Nor secret vaults to fly
>   From thunder's violence.

What I find amazing today is that, in 500 pages of poetry ranging from Chaucer to the 1940s I could possibly have picked out that one. And what an ineffable prig I must have been to be shaping myself at that age towards an upright life and a guiltless heart! But then the poem is pure Marcus Aurelius. The second page reference makes it clear that I wasn't finding the path to virtue an easy ride. It is to a poem by Sir Philip Sidney. The last line is heavily underscored with exclamation marks in the margin. It reads:

> Desiring nought but how to kill desire.

So that rounds off the picture. I was crippled by lust at the age of fifteen and my chances of harmless joys were slim.

There were not many chances, it must be said, of the other kind of joys for a teenager in the late 1940s. The predominant sexual ethos, now preserved only in period novels, was that sexual activity was appropriate only between married adults of the opposite sex. In practice this worked out that girls would hold out for as long as possible, and if they gave way and became pregnant – which commonly followed before the Pill – then they would expect to marry the man and settle down to have a family.

I had a long and intimate relationship with one girl through my teenage years. We were both involved in acting, intensely romantic and high-minded. We might well have read the Thomas Campion poem together, but I would never have shown her the one by Sidney. We exchanged vows to save ourselves for each other until our wedding night. We read, and wrote, poems expressing our passion. Mine, I remember, were full of hopeless yearning, because all my poetry was derivative and the yearning ones had the best ring to them. We specially loved Rupert Brooke and I, above all, the poem which begins:

> Breathless, we flung us on the windy hill,
>   Laughed in the sun and kissed the lovely grass.
> You said, 'Through glory and ecstasy we pass . . .

It goes on:

> 'We are Earth's best, that learnt her lesson here.
> Life is our cry. We have kept the faith,' we said . . .

and ends

>   Proud we were
>   And laughed, that had such brave true things to say
>   – And then you suddenly cried, and turned away.

That final note of anguish, inseparable, it seemed to me, from true love.

I allowed the irrational passion of love to intrude into an otherwise rational life because I was spending my days and nights studying literature, and so much literature was driven by it. We had *A Midsummer Night's Dream* and the poems of Keats for Eng. Lit., while in French the set book was something called *Nine French Poets*, including Victor Hugo, Alfred de Musset and Lamartine, with lots of sitting about on wet black rocks in the mountains and moaning into the mists. Even a stolidly unemotional working-class lad from Yorkshire had to be affected.

The study of French was a profound culture shock for me. I loved the sound of the words and, having some talent for mimicry, enjoyed speaking them. I went to all the French films that came to our local arts cinema in Bradford and took to listening at home to broadcasts in French on the radio – especially if there was a chance I might be discovered doing so. When I was fifteen, I decided I should go to France to see if the French really lived as they did in the films. My parents were not keen. The French were dirty and badly brought up. There were dark rumours about their not using toilet paper. Anyway, we could not afford the fares. But I decided to go and, having saved enough from my paper-round money to pay the ferry, I set off to hitchhike to the coast 200 miles away. I packed some sandwiches in a carrier bag and waved goodbye to Mam from the farmyard gate. I remember she waved back and said to my brothers, 'He'll be back in a couple of hours.' I decided to show she was wrong.

I am telling this story now not to celebrate my juvenile intrepidity but because the trip led to a strange experience. I had no trouble getting to Normandy, where I was given work on a farm for a couple of weeks before setting off for Paris. The farmer had told me to sleep under the bridges with the *clochards*, but I met a kind policeman who offered to lock me away every night in a cell, releasing me at dawn before the inspector called.

I went to the Louvre, and there it happened. I should say now that my visual sense has always been my weakest. Of the visual arts, sculpture always appealed more than painting, perhaps because, being three-dimensional, its effect was better able to make an impact on my dull sensibilities. I had studied the history of painting as part of an attempt at turning myself into a Cultured Person, and could probably have rattled off a list of the great artists from Giotto to Cézanne. But no paintings really moved me apart, perhaps, from a frisson of erotic pleasure at the Rokeby Venus. So I went to the Louvre because it was unthinkable for a fifteen-year-old aspiring intellectual to visit Paris without doing so. I disliked art galleries and should much have preferred to study a book of reproductions in the privacy of home, but I thought I might get some mild satisfaction from ticking off the paintings I had come across in my *History of the World's Great Artists*.

The place was as boring as I expected, and I strolled along the lines of paintings at a fairly brisk pace because there was a lot of ground to cover. And then I came face to face with Leonardo's *Virgin of the Rocks*. The impact was immediate and physical. I felt as if an external force had suddenly compressed my solar plexus and forced the breath out of my body. I remember feeling faint, sinking on to a bench and sitting in front of the painting staring at it. Not at any particular detail at first, but at the whole painting taken in at once. And then I felt drawn into it, that I could touch the shrubs and flowers in the background and smell the wet rocks. It was not a feeling of pure pleasure, rather of high tension, and it must have lasted for about half an hour. I had never previously had such a feeling, and I can still remember it quite clearly.

The experience was not entirely pleasant but I wanted to repeat it, and when I heard some years later that the National Gallery in London had a copy of the painting I made a special trip to see it. But nothing happened. I later learned that the National Gallery version was partly from the hand of a pupil, but I can hardly imagine that my artistic sensibilities were detecting inferior workmanship. Perhaps these things just don't happen twice.

Although I had problems in responding to the visual arts, I developed a strong passion for music. There had always been song in the house, because my mother loved singing and would teach me, as we washed up together, gems from Gilbert and Sullivan and Rudolf Friml. Then, for a Christmas present, I think, somebody gave me a twelve-inch red-label HMV record of Gigli singing 'O Paradiso!' on one side and 'M'apparì' on the other. I decided that if this was classical music I wanted more of it.

This was difficult at home, because our radio was taboo to the children. We were not allowed to touch it. My father always listened to the news and believed that if anyone ever changed the wavelengths they would never reassemble themselves properly inside the set again. It was quite an old wireless with, above the glass panel that showed the stations, a Gothic design depicting a mermaid swimming with one hand to her ear and above her a scroll bearing the words 'What Are the Wild Waves Saying?' Occasionally the set misbehaved by crackling or suddenly falling silent, and my father responded as he did to mischief in his children by whacking it with the flat of his hand. This always worked, though if we ever tried it he would shout, 'It's *them*. Don't touch it. It's *them*.' 'Them' was the BBC.

I did make a crystal set from a kit, but the reception always seemed to combine two or more stations. But one day a friend at the grammar school asked me if I would like a job selling programmes for the concerts of classical music held in Huddersfield Town Hall. There were no wages, but the programme-sellers were allowed free seats. So I got to hear John Barbirolli and the Hallé Orchestra, The Huddersfield Choral Society, Sergiu Celibidache, Sir Thomas Beecham. The last triggered off another unforgettable experience which affected me permanently.

Peter France

It was a Saturday-evening concert with the Royal Philharmonic Orchestra. I had managed to be first in the queue to cash up by handing in my unsold programmes and the money at the desk backstage, so as to miss as little as possible of the music. I ran round to the front of house and upstairs to the circle, bursting through the door just as Sir Thomas Beecham's baton swept down and the orchestra exploded into the first four blazing chords of the prelude to *The Mastersingers*. What then happened I find hard to describe, because for a few seconds I lost normal consciousness. I remember a surge of wonder pulsating through my body. It was not entirely pleasurable; there was a tinge of panic in it. I was aware only of the music, and desperately wanted it to go on and on. I sat on the steps transfixed until the overture ended. And after the concert I wanted to have again the experience that overture had triggered off in me. I looked for the prelude to *The Mastersingers* and even bought, many years later, a recording made by Sir Thomas Beecham with the RPO, but the sensation never returned. What happened that night was a unique experience, but it had the power I later learned to associate, in others, with a religious experience. It was what Ada Hopper had called 'joy'.

Chapter Two

When the time came to think about a university we had a family crisis. My mother was resigned to having me spend another three years reading books, though their effect on my character had been exactly what she had feared all along: I was known in the village as half-daft. The only university she, or I, had thought of was at Leeds, only twelve miles away. Enrolled there, I should be able to live at home and stay within the unyielding cultural embrace of Yorkshire. This, for Yorkshire people, is just about as necessary as breathing. In fact the folklore of our village, maintained by a selective community memory, was that nobody born there had ever left it – in the sense of abandoning it for ever. All Cliftoners, it was said, ended up in Clifton. But Rastrick Grammar School had acquired a new English master who had been to Oxford University, and he thought that I should have a go at following him there. This caused the crisis.

I have a vivid recollection of sitting in the kitchen while Dad and Mam argued. She was – and this rarely happened – in tears. 'If he goes to Oxford we shall lose him,' she wailed. 'Leeds was good enough for everybody else. Why isn't it good enough for our Pete?' Dad was firm. 'He'll go as far as he can go,' he said, 'and I'll not stand in his way.' The coal fire flickered on the blackened hearth and my mother sat at the scrubbed table with her head in her worn hands mourning the loss of her third son to the soft allurements of the South. The episode reruns itself occasionally in my memory with all the emotional intensity of a scene from a novel by D. H. Lawrence. In fact, come to think of it, perhaps it is a scene from a novel by D. H. Lawrence.

The school entered me for an Oxford open scholarship at the Christ Church/Magdalen/New College group of colleges. Nobody expected me to win it, but there was a dim hope that I might do well enough to be offered a place by one of them. I went to Oxford to sit the examination and was immediately floored by an incident on the first evening. The candidates were all staying in Christ Church, and I had met there a seventeen-year-old public schoolboy who suggested that we go out for a drink. I called at his rooms as arranged, feeling very bucked that a public schoolboy should have chosen to spend time with me. As I knocked on the door, he called cheerfully from inside, 'Hang on a minute. I'll just give my face a perfunctory dab.'

I was dismayed. What right had I to be in the same building, the same college, sitting the same competitive examination as somebody with such a vocabulary? I had never met anyone who could have spoken such words. I had a fair idea of what 'perfunctory' meant; it would not have thrown me if I'd come across it in a book. But to have somebody of my own age carelessly toss such a phrase in my direction – and a rival in the coming examination! I knew I was hopelessly out of my depth and didn't cheer up all evening, although my new friend spent the time assuring me that he had only come to Oxford for a jaunt and had no hope of ever passing anything.

I didn't win the scholarship; but I did manage to satisfy, or perhaps to arouse the curiosity of, the examiners enough for them to offer me a place. When the news came, I was serving my Queen and Country. As a Yorkshireman, I elected to do my national service with our county regiment, the Green Howards. So the army posted me to Wales – to The Welch Regiment at Dering Lines, Brecon – and gave me a bed in Hut 23 with eighteen lads from the valleys and one from Deal in Kent.

The army brings you up against the ultimates: you are trained, after all, to kill and to avoid being killed. And, although we had no expectation of being put at greater risk than twisting an ankle on the assault course, we all had to face the solemnity of filling in the identity forms which contained spaces for 'NEXT OF KIN' and 'RELIGION'. These were kept as records should the worst happen. The corporal in charge of our hut was there to help us fill in the forms. In the space for 'RELIGION', having by that time thought and read a deal about the matter, I wrote in a well-considered 'NONE'. The corporal called me into his room and told me that the word 'None' was not in the list of options for this space. You have to write, he explained patiently, 'Methodist', 'Baptist', 'R.C.' and so on. But such things were important to me at eighteen years old and I felt the need to insist on absolute honesty, especially on a document that was going to be consulted in the event of my sudden death. I told him firmly and clearly that I had no faith, that I did not believe in anything. 'Ah, then,' he said equally firmly, 'you have to put "C. of E." '

And so the army classified us. There were the chapel lads, miners from the valleys, and a few 'R.C.s' who had to be released on Sundays to attend Mass because otherwise they would go to hell. We thought of them as being attached to some Italian cult, because their services were in Latin and they worshipped the Pope. Then there were the rest – the vast impious horde registered as part of the body of our national church: the 'C. of E.', assembled in serried ranks for church parade when the flags would be unfurled and the colonel would lead us in 'Soldiers of Christ, arise; And put your armour on'; 'Stand up – stand up for Jesus! Ye soldiers of the Cross'; and, of course 'Onward, Christian soldiers!' and 'Fight the good fight'. I was not a pacifist, but I found it hard to understand how these military men could have their banners blessed by a parson who represented the Prince of Peace. And I remembered my father's knock-down proof of the falsity of religion which came from his experience in the

First World War. Both sides were praying for victory to the same God, he told me, and they swapped mince pies in no man's land on his son's birthday before crawling back into their trenches on Boxing Day and doing their best to kill each other again.

I was at Dering Lines when a letter came from my ex-headmaster, telling me of the offer of a place at New College. I remember the delight of having made it to Oxford being tarnished by being accepted only at what I took to be a modern annexe, tacked on to the ancient seat of learning. I supposed that the older foundations were peopled by public schoolboys and that only an upstart calling itself 'New' would open its doors to grammar-school boys. (The Brecon public library was able to set me right, as I found there a reference to the establishment of New College by William of Wykeham in 1379.)

But the headmaster's congratulatory letter had a traumatic sequel which has never left my memory. I answered with a polite note of gratitude to him and to the school. I spent a little time over it. It was elegant, if a touch florid, and I remember reading it with a feeling of pleasure that I could occasionally express myself with style if I spent enough time polishing. I stuck down the envelope with a definite self-assurance that, having been accepted at Oxford, I had cleared life's final fence. And then a hurdle loomed: I realized that I did not know how to address it. My etiquette books were clear and helpful on sending communications to archbishops, Cabinet ministers, the Queen or the Pope. But they were silent on the topic of headmasters. I could not work out whether I should call him 'Esq.' or 'Mr'. So I put both. Just to be sure.

He did take the trouble to reply. And his words are burned into my memory. He thanked me for my letter and added that he assumed the conflict between the toxins and anti-toxins in my bloodstream – the course of injections given to all new recruits – had caused me to address him as 'Mr E. J. S. Kyte Esq.' 'I make', he added simply, 'no further

comment.' He made no further comment because he wanted
to save me the embarrassment of being told the obvious.
After all, everybody knew how to address an envelope. Mine
was a solecism which required no more than a raised
eyebrow, like an unbuttoned fly.

This observation, kindly meant, of my headmaster, rankled
with me for years. Nobody in my family circle happened to
have come by the knowledge of how to address an envelope,
and so I could not have picked up at home what everybody
was supposed to know. I had tried to overcome my social
insecurity by reading all the books on etiquette I could find; I
had committed to memory a complex web of arcane practices
ranging from turning down the corner of a visiting-card to
eating asparagus, but still there were areas of behaviour
where I could be caught out. And these were in the small
details that I would have to face every day. I fed my paranoia
with imaginings that the middle-classes taught their children
in secret how 'well-bred' people behaved, so that upstarts like
myself would give themselves away. I find amongst my notes
on good behaviour nervously preserved from this time the
following unsettling para:

> A solecism may be perhaps in itself but a trifling matter,
> but in the eyes of society at large it assumes proportions of a
> magnified aspect and reflects most disadvantageously upon
> the one by whom it is committed; the direct inference being
> that to be guilty of a solecism argues the offender to be
> unused to society and consequently not on an equal footing
> with it. This society resents and is not slow in making its
> disapproval felt by its demeanour towards the offender.

The army was a great relief for the social paranoiac. We all
wore the same clothes and were forced into the same insane
rituals, like scraping the barrack-room table with razor
blades and rubbing polish into our boots with hot spoons.
Since no recruit of sound mind had ever done anything like
this in his previous life, we were all learning our military
behavioural code from scratch. In English regiments, no

doubt, the subtleties of regional accent and vocabulary would allow class differences to assert themselves, even in the enforced uniformity of the first six weeks of basic training. But I was with the Welsh.

There was one other non-Welsh lad in our barrack room. His name was Andrew Tilley; he was from a minor public school in Kent and had played rugby for his county's junior side. He was big and tough, but when he enthused about anything his eyes went pink and moist and he dribbled with excitement. He loved beer and poetry. We became close friends. On free weekends we would climb to a place called Cwm Llwch on the slopes of Pen-y-Fan mountain and scramble through the window of a deserted shepherd's cottage there to spread our sleeping bags on the floor and spend most of the nights reciting poetry and discussing God and love and food and masturbation. We didn't really know much about the first three. The food conversations were mainly about quantity. Love, I remember, we agreed was essential because it made you feel intensely, and intense feelings were the best things in life. On the whole it was best unrequited, because all the best poems were about that – and, anyway, requited love led to marriage and home and children and middle age.

Poetry was exciting at the most basic sensual level, because of the physical effects it had on us. We rated it like electricity, in terms of voltages. We tried out lines on each other to see whether the hair prickled at the back of the neck:

For he on honey-dew hath fed,
And drunk the milk of Paradise . . .

There midnight's all a-glimmer, and noon a purple glow,
And evening full of the linnet's wings . . .

　　Time held me green and dying
Though I sang in my chains like the sea.

This was the 'White Goddess' approach to poetry. Robert Graves had suggested that the ancient goddess of poetry was the goddess of the moon: the White Goddess. When you read words that make you catch your breath slightly or experience that sense of the numinous which cannot be analysed, that current of feeling like a charge of electricity, then She had been present at the act of creation. It was an inspiring idea, and we tried it out on each other. The most powerful, inexplicable – perhaps powerful because it was inexplicable – piece of English poetry, we agreed, was a mysterious passage in Donne:

> When I am gone, dream me some happiness,
> Nor let thy looks our long-hid love confess,
> Nor praise, nor dispraise me, nor bless nor curse
> Openly love's force, nor in bed fright thy Nurse
> With midnights startings crying out, oh, oh
> Nurse, oh my love is slain, I saw him go
> O'er the white Alps alone . . .

Through the cottage window at Cwm Llwch in the Brecon Beacons we could see the peak of Pen-y-Fan and we talked about the words of Psalm 121: 'I will lift up mine eyes unto the hills, from whence cometh my help.' We had both experienced, and were to experience together, the raising of the spirits you feel when looking up at mountain peaks, especially if you're climbing among them. We would not have put it down to God, because God – at least the Christian God – was the Great Denier, harnessed by the meaner human spirits to keep down soaring enthusiasms of all kind with the promise that, if this life were miserable enough, the next would be better. I remember from those times a Dorothy Parker quatrain:

> Whose love is given over-well
> Shall look on Helen's face in hell,
> Whilst they whose love is thin and wise
> May view John Knox in paradise.

We were raring to head for Helen. Our wild oats were sprouting and over-ready for the sowing. But these were the chaste 1940s, and there was nowhere to broadcast them. At least, Tilley and I, strutting the Brecon streets in crisp new uniforms with haircuts that showed the pink-white flesh vulnerable under our caps, never found anywhere. Perhaps a few of the 1,200 other new recruits who strutted the same streets were luckier. We were happy enough to postpone the Great Initiation. In our imaginations our sexual ambitions were global: the world, with all its women, was our oyster. Though had we been confronted at the time with an available woman – or oyster – we should not have had the faintest idea how to proceed.

For Tilley, the important things in life were passion and spontaneity. The enemies to be routed were seemliness and moderation. We shared this scale of values. I no longer remember who contributed what. Nor do I know what part in his zest for living was played by the secret knowledge, which he never shared with me, that he had an incurable form of cancer. He died only a few years later.

I would count Tilley as the most powerful spiritual influence I came across in the army. We were always looking together over the boundary fence of military activities into the world where things mattered. In the bustle and boredom of a daily routine of square-bashing, assault courses, target practice and naming of parts we would see the blossoms, fragile and motionless, and the early bees assaulting the flowers and easing the spring. That poetry could be important, perhaps even the most important thing in life, to a powerful, broken-nosed, beer-drinking, energetically heterosexual rugby forward was a revelation and a reassurance to me.

I had an inglorious army career. My friends went to fight in Korea, and some came back with medals. I wanted above all to travel, so I listed in my preferences for postings (1) the Far East, (2) the Middle East and (3) Germany. I was in consequence sent to Catterick Camp in Yorkshire, where I spent the rest of my military career producing plays in the garrison theatre, mainly for the benefit of the major-general's daughter, who was an enthusiastic amateur actress.

I went up to Oxford about five years too soon. In 1956 John Osborne's play *Look Back in Anger* was to be an immense success and suddenly everybody wanted to be working-class. The middle classes were out, and 'real people', for a time, were the ones who ate bread and dripping, lived in back-to-back cottages, and despised the posh Sunday papers. The aristocracy of this social revolution was the miners and their families: scruffy clothes, designer stubble and regional accents were *de rigueur*. If only I had gone up later I should have joined the cream: my working-class qualifications were impeccable.

But I arrived in New College in October 1951, and felt immediately lost. Back into civilian clothes, I had to face the nightmare of choosing them. College was intimidating: my rooms were swept by a man old enough to be my father, so I felt I should be cleaning up for him; we sat for dinner at long, black oak tables and were served by college servants in stiff white coats; anyone guilty of certain solecisms at table could be 'sconced' – made to down two and a half pints of college ale at a draught. I should have enjoyed the challenge of the ale, but not under the eyes of the entire college and for having said or done something socially maladroit. It didn't happen, but I always ate in a personal cloud of anxiety that it might.

The other students – mainly middle-class, mainly public school – were unfailingly helpful and supportive. But the problem was that they treated me as one of themselves, which I wasn't. I very much wanted to have that same casual air of confidence in all situations which is the most precious gift of our great educational institutions, but it wouldn't come. I know that the anxieties I felt were unnecessary and self-induced; that the chip I carried on my shoulder was all my own work; that my fellow students did not give a damn about the social niceties which made me feel inadequate.

They were always ready to accept me. I rejected them, and slunk around the streets of Oxford in army-surplus clothes hoping not to be noticed.

But in one small area of student activities I was completely confident – the theatre. By this time I had experience acting with local professional repertory companies, I had an Actors' Equity union ticket and spent my vacations playing bit parts at theatres in Bradford, Huddersfield and Halifax. I began producing college play-readings and then college plays, and then moved into the Oxford University Dramatic Society, where I found security. This last move was the most relevant to my spiritual education, though I did not realize it at the time, because of one man: Neville Coghill.

The OUDS had a reputation for brilliant productions involving professional actors. The most legendary of all is that of *The Tempest* in the grounds of Worcester College in the summer of 1949, when Caliban emerged miraculously from the waters of the lake and Ariel scuttered across the surface supported by a system of duckboards just beneath the water. The production was by Neville Coghill, who, at the time I became secretary of OUDS, was its patron.

He was a tutor in English at Exeter College, and we used to meet in his rooms there from time to time to talk about productions. I knew of him as the translator of the Penguin edition of *The Canterbury Tales*, and remember feeling sightly embarrassed at meeting the man responsible for making available to the general public the coarse language and uproarious obscenities of 'The Miller's Tale'.

The first time I met him he impressed me because some point came up about Shakespeare's career and he leaned over and took out *The Oxford Companion to English Literature* to look it up. It is a measure of my naivety that I found this surprising: firstly that he didn't know the answer, and secondly that he was so ready to reveal to a junior student that he didn't know it. And, as I came to know him, I realized that he rarely divulged that he knew anything at all. He was always so interested to hear what I had to say that he would lean forward in his chair, nod enthusiastically, and make only such comment as would encourage me to go on talking. Later, much later, I came to understand that this is true humility. And that Neville Coghill was a Christian.

The ethos of Oxford was not one to encourage religious exploration. It is a commonplace of the sociology of knowledge that our views of reality are shaped by what our contemporaries find plausible. We obtain our notions about the world from other human beings, and we retain these notions so long as they have social support. This process is particularly intense and concentrated at university. At Oxford, during the time I spent there, the social pressures were against religious belief. It seemed to me – though my view was warped by the chip I was carrying – that the most important thing was to be clever. And the paradox was that, although one should have read everything, one should not be seen to spend time reading. The cream of society passed their mornings drinking coffee, their afternoons on the river and their evenings sipping sherry. Vacations were spent abroad, as evidenced by deep tans at the beginning of term or a leg in plaster at the appropriate season to indicate a skiing trip. One man turned up after the vacation that immediately preceded his final examinations with a confident bearing and a defiant tan, only to have it revealed that he had spent the time at home shut in his room with his books and a sunlamp.

Christianity was not a subject for discussion. Most of us had read Freud and, although we were sceptical about his reduction of all human drives to the sexual, we went along with his view on religion: it is an illusion, and it derives its strength from the fact that it falls in with our instinctual desires. I think we had the same attitude towards Christians as towards women or the sick: it would be ungallant to be discourteous to the frail. And Christianity proclaimed itself as the religion of the losers: to the poor and the persecuted was promised the kingdom of heaven, and the meek would inherit the earth. As Oxford students, we had no ambitions to spend our lives being poor, persecuted or meek, so the Sermon on the Mount was not for us.

The institutional Church was well established as a butt for humour. One of our national comedians complained he couldn't stand the competition from the Archbishop of Canterbury. Parsons lost their trousers on the West End stages as regularly as French windows opened to tennis-playing juvenile leads. But there was one parson who was undeniably clever, who could out-Oscar Wilde at fashionable dinner parties and who was a shining role model for any Oxford student. He became mine for a time, and I have never lost my admiration for him. Sydney Smith had a passion for good food and drink and a High Church agnosticism that allowed him to greet a friend in the street with the words 'I am just going to pray for you at St Paul's, but with no very lively hope of success.'

I think the most fundamental objection I conceived against Christianity at Oxford was that it was self-seeking and fundamentally immoral. This was, of course, a rationalization of my rejection of it, which was almost certainly because it preached standards of behaviour I was unwilling to accept. But, staying within the realms of conscious memory, I was always upset by the texts which promised rewards for good behaviour: those who keep the commandments 'shall be called great in the kingdom of heaven'; if you give alms or fast or pray in secret 'your Father who sees in secret will reward you'; but if you make a show of your piety 'you will have no reward from your Father who is in Heaven'. It seemed to me, as a flawed but idealistic twenty-one-year-old, that good behaviour should be its own reward; that a religion which bribed people to behave decently in this life so as to receive a reward in the next was a second-rate creed for the morally underdeveloped. I was able to reject Christianity from the moral high ground.

One disadvantage of my rejection of Christianity was that I found it difficult, and often impossible, to read the Christian poets who were an essential part of the English literature I was supposed to be studying. With Milton I had no problems, because of the power and sheer beauty of his poetry, and because much of it is narrative or dramatic. But the poets who sang of their Christian faith, like George Herbert, Thomas Campion and Henry Vaughan, I found unreadable because they were celebrating something which seemed to me to be a cause for lamentation. I also had a problem with allegory, again because of the infantile literalism which made me prefer encyclopaedias to novels. So the poems of Edmund Spenser, again a fundamental and unmissable part of the course, I could not read. Myths, fairy tales, legendary heroes had no charm for me, because all my passion was for people who had actually existed, events that had really happened. History was everything; tales of mystery and imagination were simply a pollution of the mind.

I had a very clear notion of the progress of human development: my view of the past was formed by prejudice and unclouded by knowledge. So I could see that, after the Dark Ages, when the civilized world had been kept in superstition and ignorance by the Church, the sun of the Renaissance had broken through and given us the glories of Italian painting and Elizabethan theatre. Then the Puritans had plunged England back into the gloom of Christianity, until science, working underground during the seventeenth century, had liberated humanity once more into the clear bright skies of the Enlightenment. But then the French Revolution had frightened the English upper classes into realizing that free thought led to the loss of their lands, houses and heads, so they became deeply religious again and Victorianism arrived.

It seemed to me that I had an unusual awareness of and sympathy for the spirit of the Renaissance – I needed to feel special about something – because of my social background. The Renaissance, after all, had been the first time when lower-class lads could rise in society. Shakespeare, like me, was the third son of a butcher; Ben Jonson was brought up by a bricklayer. More importantly, the characteristics of a gentleman, as delineated by Castiglione in one of the most popular books of the sixteenth century, *Il Cortegiano*, were not that he should be the son of a gentleman but that he was well-read, open to the beauty of the arts, an adept at physical exercises. I thought that with my studies at Rastrick Grammar, my acting of Shakespeare and my sessions with the weights over the public bar of the Rising Sun, I was in with a chance.

Also, the Renaissance had emerged from an ecclesiastical and feudal despotism into the high bright land of the free human spirit, just as I had thrown off the thrall of chapel morality and the class divisions of Clifton society to reconstitute myself as a free human being in my New College rooms. The basic change of orientation marked by the Renaissance was from an acceptance of this life as a period of trial in preparation for the next, to a joyous celebration of this life as the one to delight in. I started to read books about food and wine, so that I should know how to set about the celebrating should I ever have the cash.

It seemed to me, in my early twenties, that life should be full, exciting and brief. I was stocky, snub-nosed and healthy; but I longed to be pale, slender and interesting, with a slight stoop and haunted eyes. I even slept for some months with a clothes-peg on my nose in a desperate attempt to look like the French actor Jean-Louis Barrault. I had myself photographed in my rooms, standing by the fireplace in a borrowed jacket and tie with a bottle of gin on the mantelpiece behind me, a long cigarette-holder and what I hoped was a cynical expression. When my friends told me they stayed up until four a.m. drinking black coffee and reading decadent books, never rising before noon, I tried the regimen of the sophisticated. But the black coffee gave me indigestion, I fell asleep over the books, and I found it impossible to stay in bed after eight. And during my three years at Oxford I never discovered what absinthe was.

So I projected, for a time, the clean-limbed Rupert Brooke

image: flinging myself about breathlessly and being all tousle-haired and free:

> They love the Good; they worship Truth;
> They laugh uproariously in youth;
> (And when they get to feeling old,
> They up and shoot themselves, I'm told) . . .

The humiliations of age had to be avoided. I remembered men with expanding waistlines and sagging pectorals pumping iron at the Rising Sun and saying they 'had to hang on to what they'd got'; I could still picture my grandfather, who kept his teeth in a glass by the bed and always smelt faintly of pee. I had retained my trust in Marcus Aurelius enough to be ready to help myself out of the indignities of age, which I anticipated would come along soon after my thirtieth birthday. So, like Cleopatra, I began seriously to study the best way to go when the time came. I was not convinced by her method of being bitten by an asp, although historians record that she settled on this only after years of experiment and consultation with her doctors. Shooting seemed satisfactory, though the Hemingway method with a twelve-bore shotgun must have left a mess for somebody to clear up. On the whole, drugs seemed the least likely to be painful, and as barbiturates were cheap and readily available I made a mental note to go that way, without making any specific preparations.

Suicide was a crime. With the moral earnestness of youth, I had to discover whether it was also wrong. Marcus Aurelius had advocated it; Mark Antony had put it into practice; Shakespeare seemed to portray 'the Roman way' as a lofty ideal. There was nothing in the Ten Commandments against it, although some moral theologians extended the commandment not to kill to self-extinction. But Saul had fallen on his sword when his armour-bearer refused to kill him; Ahitophel had set his house in order and hanged himself; and Zimri burned the king's house over his own head. None of these deaths was condemned by the Old Testament writers. Admittedly, the most famous New Testament suicide was Judas, an unrecommendable role model, but there was no suggestion that what he did in hanging himself was wrong, rather that it was appropriate. So, as I could find nothing against suicide in any authority which I respected, I decided that it was a good idea when the right time came.

Suicide was, of course, condemned by the Christian Church, and suicides had been refused burial in churchyards, even being planted at crossroads to confuse their wandering darkened spirits. I took this as another instance of a benighted and superstitious institution frightening its members into toeing the line. The Christian Church had, from its origins, a genius for manipulating credulity as I learned from the often quoted, but always enjoyable winding up of the notorious Chapter 15 of *The Decline and Fall of the Roman Empire*:

> During the age of Christ, of his apostles, and of their first disciples, the doctrine which they preached was confirmed by innumerable prodigies. The lame walked, the blind saw, the sick were healed, the dead were raised, daemons were expelled, and the laws of Nature were frequently suspended for the benefit of the church. But the sages of Greece and Rome turned aside from the awful spectacle and, pursuing the ordinary occupations of life and study, appeared unconscious of any alterations in the moral or physical government of the world.

I first came across this passage in a book called *Gibbon on Christianity*, which was published by the Rationalist Press Association as part of a series called The Thinker's Library. These were small, easily assimilable volumes readily available for a few pence in second-hand bookshops, with an attractive image of Rodin's statue *Le Penseur* on the spine and cover. At this stage of my life I was beginning to think of myself as a thinker – my brothers had not been slow to point out that I didn't seem any good at anything else. I was hesitant in conversation not because I had any doubts about the value of what I had to say but because I was still not completely competent in the pronunciation of southern English. Unless I kept a careful eye on myself, I left off the aitches where we left them off in Yorkshire and – even worse – I would sometimes, through straining to avoid the guttural Yorkshire vowels and bring them to the front of the mouth, find myself saying 'bert' instead of 'but' and pronouncing 'put' to rhyme with 'hut'. As I could not present myself as having a ready wit, I decided to be silent and enigmatic in company, hoping to be thought profound. To have a row of rather serious titles on my mantelpiece would help in the projection of this image, and I managed to acquire, second-hand and for the price of a couple of pints of beer, Thomas Paine's *The Age of Reason*, J. B. S. Haldane's *Fact and Faith*, Albert Einstein's *The World As I See It*, Sir Leslie Stephen's *An Agnostic's Apology* and Julian Huxley's *Religion Without Revelation*.

The last of this list was the most influential. Huxley was a thoroughgoing evolutionist with a passionate commitment to the truth. Both aspects appealed to me. He pointed out that science had gradually replaced religion as the authority which could explain the workings of the world. First the heavenly bodies, then the construction of the earth, then the plants and animals, and the physical working of the human body, all were gradually made comprehensible by science without reference to supernatural agencies. There remained only the operation of the human mind, with its aptitude for ecstasy, awe, religious inspiration. This would be revealed in time to be an entirely natural consequence of evolutionary influences. The psychologists were hard at work.

God, like the Cheshire Cat in *Alice in Wonderland*, was gently fading away from the sight of humanity until only a faint cosmic smile remained. Yet the question of his existence or non-existence had to be tackled:

> Until it is settled, and the idea of God relegated to the past
> with the idea of ritual magic and other products of primitive

and unscientific human thought, we shall never get the new religion we need.

This new religion, which Huxley called for to satisfy humanity's basic instinct for reverence, was one in which people would recognize that they were the highest entity of which they had any knowledge, that human values were all they had, and that they must work out their salvation and destiny under their own steam. This philosophy underpinned an attitude to life which I found compelling: since this life is all we have, we should make the most of it. 'I believe first and foremost,' wrote Huxley, 'that life is not merely worth living but intensely precious; and that the supreme object of life is to live . . .' After all the cautious tiptoeing around and between temptations of the Christian life of trial, this was heady stuff, and I embraced it. I became, and began to call myself, a Humanist.

One paradoxical result of this was that I began to read the Bible carefully for the first time. I had noticed that Bernard Shaw, who routed the Christian apologists now and again, often did so by knowing his Bible better than they did. To confuse the enemy by quoting their own scriptures at them seemed an agreeable prospect. I set about the Gospels with notebook and pencil, jotting down all the unchristian bits: 'I have not come to bring peace, but a sword . . . to set man against his father and a daughter against her mother . . . He who is not with me is against me.' Jesus seems to relish the sufferings of hell for those who disagree with him: 'The angels will come out and separate the evil from the righteous, and throw them into the furnace of fire; there men will weep and gnash their teeth.'

Although many Humanists seemed, like Mr Baldwin, to preach the idea that Jesus was a highly moral person whose teaching centred on the universal precept of doing to others as you would be done by, it seemed to me that this notion could not survive a careful study of the Gospels. What are we, as leftist idealists with a strong sense of social justice, to make of the story of the vineyard owner who pays the same wages to the workers who turn up an hour before closing time as to the ones who have worked all day? Yet Jesus compares him to the kingdom of heaven. And he tells with approval the appalling story of the poor chap who turned up at the wedding wearing the wrong clothes: 'Then the king said to the attendants, "Bind him hand and foot, and cast him into the outer darkness; there men will weep and gnash their teeth."' This king is also compared to the kingdom of heaven. And what about the petty, spiteful gesture of cursing a fig tree because it failed to bear fruit when figs were not even in season?

It was evident from these stories that Jesus had no sense of social justice. And as to his divinity, insisted on by the Christians, he could hardly be divine and pray to himself, and he had made matters clear by his response to the rich young man who called him 'Good Teacher': 'Why do you call me good? No one is good but God alone.' And it is impossible to reconcile his divine nature with his having been so wrong about the future. The darkened sun, the stars falling from the heavens, the Son of Man coming in clouds with great power and glory, the hosts of angels with loud trumpet calls, all this, he stated quite unambiguously, would happen while some of his hearers were still alive. He was wrong.

My favourite incompatible verses in the Gospels, which I came across during this period of intense and critical analysis and which I used for thirty years afterwards to confound the biblical fundamentalists, were Matthew 10:10 and Mark 6:8. Whenever I interviewed people whose faith was based on the divine inspiration of the Bible which could never err, I would triumphantly point out that, in Matthew's account of the sending out of the Apostles, Christ tells them to take no bag nor sandals nor a staff. But in Mark's account of the same incident Christ tells them quite specifically they must take a staff and they must wear sandals. Not, perhaps, an inconsistency of great moment, but a discrepancy which should not be found in a document without error.

So, by careful study of the Synoptic Gospels, I became fortified against Christianity. And if anyone had asked me at the time where the strongest case against Christianity was to be found, I should have pointed to the Gospels according to Matthew, Mark and Luke.

I think it was towards the end of my time at Oxford that I heard on the radio a broadcast of T. S. Eliot's play *Murder in the Cathedral* with Robert Donat as Becket. He had the most enchanting voice of any actor, though his asthma made it impossible for him to make a big impression with it on stage. I still remember the exact sound of his voice quietly but with emphasis speaking the lines 'Peace I leave with you; my peace I give to you; not as the world giveth, give I unto you.'

The emotional impact was powerful. It was a theatrical coup like Olivier's Lear crying 'Blow, winds, and crack your cheeks!' or Gielgud's throbbing 'O, she is warm!' in *The Winter's Tale*. The words – or was it Donat's delivery of them? – were deeply moving. I went to the Gospel of St John and read them in context, in Chapter 14. This was the beginning of a fascination with that chapter which spread to the whole of the Gospel, and which has lasted until today. The text seemed to me shot through with mystical poetry of a kind which, in spite of my impatience with mysticism, touched a chord.

I have mentioned that I had a hard time with myths and legends. The rich imaginative world of fiction was not for me. And yet that chapter, although for me fictional, I found captivating from that first time I sat down to read it as an adult. 'I am the way, the truth, and the life . . . Have I been with you so long, and yet you do not know me, Philip? He who has seen me has seen the Father . . . I will not leave you desolate: I will come to you . . . Let not your hearts be troubled.' To me, these words were a sort of myth, in that I did not believe that Jesus Christ had spoken them, and yet I found them disturbing and exciting. As I read further in the Gospel, I was captivated by the imagery with which a supernatural reality explains itself to a human audience: bread, water, light, life, shepherd, door. The basic theme, that the Word was made flesh and dwelt among us full of grace and truth, I decided was one of the most beautiful myths ever to spring from the imagination of man. I had rejected Christianity because its claims were based on an illusion and its effects were a blight on the full life; but I remained a closet reader of St John's Gospel, and justified this to myself by feeling that it probably gave me the same sort of pleasure that others found in Don Quixote or Huckleberry Finn.

The only completely irrational activity I remember regularly indulging in at Oxford was listening to music. I had a close friend who shared my tastes, and we met regularly in my room or his and drank cheap wine lying on the carpet and listening to records. I remember that this was accepted in college as a taboo time, almost like a religious activity, which it was not done to interrupt. If anyone called, we would motion him to the wine bottle, and he (uninvited guests had to be male) would pour himself a glass and sit in silence until the record came to an end. If it ended, as records often did in those days, before the end of the work, we would not say anything to each other until the work was completed. This, I think, was not an affectation of artistic sensibility but a recognition that something was happening, a communication was going on, the atmosphere created by the music was not to be broken.

I think I was probably hoping to experience again the pangs of pleasure I had felt on first hearing the prelude to *The Mastersingers* in Huddersfield, but it never happened. The closest I came to that was a feeling of a rather dreamy, transported quality which was far less intense but had the merit of being repeatable. This would often happen during the adagio movement of Beethoven's Ninth Symphony, and I remember a feeling of excitement at the possibility that we were tinkering with the ineffable. Sleeve notes tended to refer

to the high spirituality of the movement, and the distinguished critic Donald Tovey had written that 'The slow
movement is beauty of an order too sublime for a world of
action; it has no action and its motion is that of the stars in
their courses . . .'

Browsing in Blackwell's bookshop one day in late 1953, I
came across a new publication of essays by the most eminent
living British composer, Ralph Vaughan Williams. It caught
my eye because of the title – 'Some Thoughts on Beethoven's
Choral Symphony' – and I turned over the pages to pick up
new insights into the significance of the adagio, which I,
following the lead of generations of critics, had decided was
the most inspiring music ever written. Vaughan Williams
calls it a *morceau de salon* and goes on to describe music
which I had thought morally uplifting as 'the Beethoven who
made strong men with whiskers brush away a silent tear'.

I felt personally humiliated. At twenty-two, I was no longer
young enough to know everything and yet not old enough
not to care. I had heard by then a fairly wide range of music
and felt secure in admitting it to a high priority in the
experiences life had to offer. But I was insecure in my tastes
and was suddenly faced with the possibility that all those
hours of listening to 'great music' were a waste of time. I had
been encouraged to feel that music had a content which was
educational, inspirational, spiritually enriching. I had come
to accept that, in some ill-defined way, lying around on a
carpet and listening to music was more 'improving' than
lying around on a carpet and not listening to music. As I was
anxious for self-improvement, I had to find out whether or
not I was wasting my time. I launched into some heavy
reading and note-taking to find the answer.

Beethoven was reputed to have said that 'Music is a higher
revelation than all wisdom and all philosophy.' There was a
general agreement that the Third, Fifth, Seventh and Ninth
symphonies were more significant than the Second, Fourth
Sixth and Eighth because they dealt with greater issues.
Beethoven's mission, wrote one critic, 'was to elevate the

instrumental forms and especially the symphony into a position where they were capable of expressing the profoundest ideas and sentiments of which the human mind was capable'. But he did not go on to explain what those ideas were – possibly taking refuge in the common saying that 'The only part of music that really matters is the part that you cannot write about.'

Stravinsky was famous for having written in his autobiography that 'music is powerless to express anything at all', but he had included in his Charles Eliot Norton lectures at Harvard the words: 'the profound meaning of music and its essential aim . . . is to promote a communion, a union of man with his fellow men and with the Supreme Being'. And then there was the letter of Mendelssohn:

> People usually complain that music is so ambiguous; that it is so doubtful what they ought to think when they hear it, whereas everyone understands words. With me it is exactly the opposite . . . The thoughts which are expressed to me by a piece of music which I love are not too indefinite to be put into words but, on the contrary, too definite.

Clearly there was a mystery here. Everyone agreed that music was more than just form. There had to be a content, an element which the composer sought to commit to music and the performers to express. Without this, music was simply a decorative art and I should take as much profit from gazing at the wallpaper as from listening to a symphony. And yet all the musical criticism I read dealt not with what the composer had to say but how well or badly he set about saying it. Perhaps the final comment on the content of music was that of Claude Lévi-Strauss: 'Music is the only language with the contradictory attributes of being at once intelligible and untranslatable.'

My own experience was that I felt I had been changed by music: that I was not the same person as I would have been had I not heard Mozart, Bach, Beethoven. The critic Percy

Scholes once wrote something to the effect that music will not save your soul but it will make your soul worth saving. And, although at the time I did not accept that I had a soul, I thought I knew what he meant.

I was married in Oxford the week following the final examinations. My bride had auditioned successfully for the part of Jessica in *The Merchant of Venice*, which I had produced in the cloisters of New College during my first term there, and from that time the breathless flinging on the windy hills of Yorkshire was behind me. We held the reception in a meadow by the river, and the guests arrived, bearing their bottles, by punt. It was a glorious day and crowned a period of my life which had at the time, and more so in retrospect, a dream-like quality. The years at Oxford never seemed a part of life but a diversion from it, as if I had turned aside from the mainstream and spent three years meandering through gentle sunlit by-waters heading in no particular direction. Perhaps the most precious gift Oxford gave me – one which I cherish and has remained with me – was the capacity to be idle.

To confront immediately the challenge of a serious career seemed precipitous, so my wife and I decided to take a year off before settling down. We would visit Guernsey, one of the Channel Islands, for a few weeks, and then work our way on to the Bordeaux region of France in time to get jobs with the grape harvest. On the first day in Guernsey I saw a notice in a camera shop in St Peter Port saying that they were looking for a photographer and would pay good wages. I had never used a camera but had kept my faith in books, so I went round to the local library and read a couple on the Art of Photography before presenting myself that evening in the shop.

The manager seemed unimpressed by my talk of *f*-numbers, shutter speeds and depth of focus. He told me he was just looking for somebody to go round the beaches and point a camera at the tourists. All I had to do was take as many snaps as possible, hand the snappees a numbered slip of paper, and move on. People can't resist calling in at the shop later to see themselves, and, when they do, 98 per cent of them buy, no matter how inexpert the shot.

I hired a bicycle and spent happy days pestering holiday-makers and learning that you can always rely on a cheerful response if you point the camera at the young children and avoid their mothers. I was set to be a blistering nuisance to the tourists of Guernsey for the entire summer when I saw a notice giving the programme of the Guernsey Repertory Company for the season and registered that the following week it was doing *Seagulls Over Sorrento* followed by *The Barretts of Wimpole Street*.

I knew that the two plays shared an unusual feature which could be to my advantage: they need more players than a resident repertory company can afford to keep on the strength. So I called round at the theatre and offered to help out doing a small part. As I had an Equity card and wasn't asking for a permanent job, the producer, Roy Dotrice, welcomed me and offered me the bit parts of Jock in *Seagulls* and Septimus in *Barretts*. We got on immediately, and after a week of swapping experiences about the seedier side of life in rep I was promoted from Septimus to the lead, Robert Browning, in *Barretts* and invited to join the company.

So I handed in my camera and said farewell to the outdoor life. The following year was taken up with a routine which involved opening a new play each Monday evening and starting rehearsals the next morning for the following week's play. Every morning was spent rehearsing, every afternoon learning words, and every evening performing another play. On Saturday night, after the performance, the entire cast would buckle down and break up the set, carrying the furniture into a warehouse next door and lowering the flats through a trapdoor to a cellar beneath the stage, where the scenic artist would set to work by about three a.m. He had to 'flat out' – paint white – the entire set, so that it would dry in time for him to redecorate it as the following week's set on

Sunday afternoon and night ready for dress rehearsal Monday morning and opening Monday night. It was not a routine allowing for leisure time; learning a new part every week took up all the brain space available; that year on Guernsey turned out to be a time of spiritual stasis.

But weekly repertory, although taxing – even 'extending' in the language of Lord Reith, who believed that all young people should be extended – was not ultimately satisfying. We went back to London in search of a job. I still wanted, above all things, to travel, and the call of the South Seas, implanted by the records of Wilfred Smith in Clifton, was faintly tugging when I realized that the Fiji islands, which are almost as far away from England as it is possible to go on the surface of the planet without starting to come back, were a British colony. Further, a best-selling book called *A Pattern of Islands*, by a colonial governor, Sir Arthur Grimble, had painted a hilarious and yet romantic picture of the life of a district officer in this, the remotest corner of the Empire. I pulled together my references and wrote to the Colonial Office for an interview.

I should have heeded the dark suits. Eight sombre men clad in them sat in a semicircle and quizzed me about my views on life and politics. I had never been able to muster what is called 'an intelligent interest in current affairs' and there was no time in weekly rep to read newspapers. So I had swotted up on the *Manchester Guardian Weekly* to find out what was going on in the world and had a wide, if inconsequential, notion of global activities. I think things were going rather well as we told each other rather severe things about the Russians.

But when they asked me how many lectures I attended each week at Oxford and I replied 'none', on the ground that they tended to be inaudible and all the lecturers had written books which could be studied in the comfort of one's rooms, the atmosphere started to thicken. One member of the panel, I remember, countered by telling me that the previous candidate had told them he regularly attended three lectures a week, to which I foolishly replied, though amiably enough, 'He was probably lying.' Everybody looked hard at the file in front of him.

The letter arrived next day. It said that, on the whole, the panel felt my abilities unsuited to Her Majesty's Colonial Administration and wished me well in my career elsewhere. I had just finished reading it when the phone rang. It was a man called Ian Thomson, who had been a member of the Colonial Office panel, asking me to a lunch of sandwiches in Hyde Park.

Ian Thomson was the only member of the panel who was a practising colonial administrator. He was serving in Fiji. He told me that he disagreed with the panel's assessment; that he could not reverse it, but that he thought he could arrange for me to be offered a four-year contract in Fiji as second-best. This would mean that I would miss out on the Devonshire course – twelve months at Cambridge learning law, administration and the Fijian language – and that I should not be a permanent and pensionable officer but would have to leave after four years. But it was a chance to get to Fiji, and I took it.

Chapter Three

I arrived in Fiji with a strong sense of mission: to rescue the Fijians from the prejudices and misjudgements of the British elite, the members of the Colonial Administrative Service. They had rejected me as not up to standard, so I would line up with the underdogs.

I felt comfortable allying myself with the Fijians. Nothing in my nature or nurture had prepared me to be a member of a ruling class, and, although a certain deftness with examination questions had qualified me to be a temporary member of the colonial administration, I was not acculturated into effortless superiority. It was far more common in the history of the Empire than I realized that the colonial officers who spent their lives in country stations should fight for the interests of the local people against the dictates of the administrators in the capital. There was nothing unusual in the attitude I took; what was perhaps odd was the fact that I arrived with it, and that its origins lay not in the experience of perceived inefficiencies but in the class consciousness and prejudices which I had developed.

My initial view of Fijians, coloured as it was by these prejudices, saw them as the working-class of Fiji; the Europeans were the middle- and upper-classes. I was, fortuitously, at the top of the heap, as District Officer and Queen's Representative. Among my ex-officio duties were those of Magistrate, Commissioner for Oaths, Justice of the

Peace, Inspector of Prisons, Controller of Customs, Receiver of Wrecks . . . The Union Jack flew outside my house, but my loyalties lay with the masses. The first thing I had to do was to learn their language, and, having arrived without the benefit of the year's tuition of the Devonshire course, I was at a disadvantage in this when compared to my contemporaries. But I knew that I had a fairly agile brain and a talent for mimicry, so I was confident of catching up.

One of the prisoners in the station jail was a schoolteacher called Pau who had been given eighteen months for some overly explicit sexual education in a remote island school. I met him on my first Saturday-morning round as Inspector of Prisons and asked if he would teach me Fijian. He was happy to agree to be released at six o'clock every morning to give me an hour's lesson before breakfast. He set me simple exercises which I would deliver each afternoon to the jail (it was only a hundred yards from my house). He corrected them and brought them to the following morning's lesson.

I was always very much better at the pronunciation than the grammar. Having been raised in weekly repertory theatre, where the qualification for a job used to be 'four accents and three suits', I had an ear for the sounds of language which was far better than my ability to understand the grammar and syntax. And, being taught by a Fijian instructor, the first sounds I heard in the language were the sounds which he made and which I imitated. This was to cause disquiet in the local European population. My boss, the District Commissioner, was approached one day in Morris Hedstrom's store by the manager, an Australian who had spent twenty years in the colony, who said, 'You should keep an eye on young France. I heard him in the store the other day trying to speak Fijian *like the Fijians*.' When the DC told me the story, without comment, I realized that there were two ways of speaking Fijian: the native way and the way of the Europeans, who, after all, learned it from each other. To attempt to speak like a Fijian was to 'go native', and this was not acceptable.

But I had decided that I would be closer to the Fijians than any other district officer they had ever had. I belonged, after all, to an exploited class, like them. I refused to travel on the government boat, the *Adi Beti*, a fine white motor launch which flew the national flag, had a smartly turned out crew and was known to all the coastal villages. Instead, I would charter a local fourteen-foot fishing-boat and conduct my tours with an interpreter and the boat's owner. I would dress, like them, in torn khaki shorts and a mud-stained sweatshirt. I never wore shoes on tour. I always arrived unannounced, and insisted on eating my meals, Fijian style, on the mat.

This was crass and insensitive behaviour. Over generations, Fijians had worked out a way to cope with district officers. This involved elaborate greeting ceremonies which allowed them to get the pigs out of the village, throw up the statutory toilets, and put right any minor infringements of the health regulations before the inspection. The formalities of speech and behaviour which seemed to me offensively servile were simply ways of keeping authority at a distance. To arrive unannounced, barefoot and mud-stained was not only disarming but insulting. The welcome ceremonies had to be gone through once they realized that I was the Queen's Representative, and it was arrogant and discourteous of me to turn up for them looking like a castaway from below deck.

But I wanted to get close, and the best way to get close to Fijians seemed to be to spend the nights drinking *kava* with them. This is the pounded root of a pepper plant which is mixed with water in a large wooden bowl and served in coconut cups. The cupful has to be drained at one draught. The drink has a mildly soporific effect and is sold abroad as a diuretic. I have always needed a lot of sleep, and found the long sessions of drinking and listening to half-understood stories very hard going, but I had a reputation to create and keep up. So I kept at it. The reputation followed and I managed to convince the colonial office that I could safely be allowed to make a career in Fiji.

As well as listening to the old tales in the villages, I read all

I could find on Fijian myth and custom as recorded by the first settlers. I made extensive notes, and compiled local histories of the stations to which I was posted. I soaked myself completely in the Fijian way of life. I was particularly interested in the tales of the supernatural. On reflection, I think that although, as a self-styled Humanist, I had rejected the supernatural in my own culture, I had a sneaking hope that traces of it might remain in a less developed one. They did.

Quite soon after I arrived in the country station of Labasa, on the island of Vanua Levu, a Public Works Department lorry stopped outside my office and a young Fijian jumped down from the cab and called for help. I saw through my window a small crowd had collected, and they lifted down from the back of the truck a sagging, twitching body. As I ran out I saw that it was the elderly Indian driver, who was pale, semiconscious and trembling. They told me that he had been hauling gravel along the coastal road when he stopped the truck by a small grove of trees and got out to relieve himself. No sooner had he started than he was seized by a fit and threw himself shaking to the ground, where he had been found by the local villagers, bundled into the truck, and driven to town. The grove of trees covered an ancient burial ground of the local chiefs.

The Fijians explained to me that this incident was a perfectly normal reaction of their buried ancestors to insult. The feature which most interested me was that the Indian driver did not know of the ancient burial ground, so his condition could not be self-induced. I took him to the hospital and asked the doctor for a diagnosis. He found nothing organically wrong with the driver, who recovered after a couple of days and went back to work. The grove of trees was respected for the rest of my time on the station.

The local god of the Fijian tribe in the area where I first worked was Dakuwaqa, the shark-god. He was reputed to have gardens in the bush, where he spent the afternoons planting and weeding before returning at night to the sea.

There were plenty of sharks in the area, and the local folklore told that they never attacked the people of this province. Dakuwaqa would not harm his own people. Since sharks did attack swimmers occasionally in other parts of Fiji, I assumed that selective memory was at work again. But there was one feature of the local behaviour I found hard to understand.

The shark has an acute sense of smell. It was long thought of as a 'swimming nose', because its other senses are far less developed. We now know that sharks have many highly sensitive abilities to detect vibration and movement, but the sense of smell, particularly for blood, is demonstrably acute. One of the occasional sports of the planters in northern Fiji used to be to tie a piece of fresh meat to the end of a jetty and then try to shoot the sharks with .45-calibre handguns as they circled. The sharks never took long to arrive, and if the blood was fresh they would sometimes make frenzied dashes at the meat, leaping and spiralling and jostling each other. It was obvious that they could detect the blood from a great distance, and that it had a powerfully energizing effect on them.

But the women in this province would often go fishing in water up to their shoulders. They would carry nets and form a circle, slowly closing in to trap the fish. Around their waists they wore cords of coconut sinnet, and as they caught the fish they would bang them on the head and string them, through the gills, along the cord. So each woman would have a circle of bleeding fish around her waist. And yet, to my amazement, they were never attacked by sharks. They themselves explained this by saying that Dakuwaqa was their god and would not harm them. I had no explanation.

The god of Koro island is possibly easier to account for. Tui Naikasi is a turtle-god, and the islanders are famous for their ceremony of calling the turtles. They assemble on a cliff top above a narrow bay and chant an appeal to the god to show himself. Usually, after a few minutes' chanting you can see in the gin-clear waters deep below the surface, a tiny yellow disc which slowly floats upwards, growing larger, and eventually breaking the surface as a turtle three feet across, its stout flippers slowly kneading the water, followed by another and another. The turtles float around for a few minutes and then slowly sink back deep out of sight. The spectacle is astonishing, and always causes great excitement. However, a marine biologist once explained to me that all turtles need to come to the surface occasionally to breathe, and that, if anyone cared to wait on the clifftop for long enough, the turtles would come whether called or not.

But the firewalking is less easy to explain away. The people of the island of Beqa were given the ability to walk on fire by one of their gods centuries ago. Today they celebrate this by digging a large pit in the ground and filling it with hardwood. They then set fire to the hardwood and place on top of it many stones, each about as large as a football. Usually they leave the fire to burn all night, so that by the morning the stones are glowing with heat. They then throw a small piece of tapa cloth on to the stones. If it immediately vanishes in a puff of smoke, the stones are ready. Wearing leaf skirts and walking slowly in single file, the men cross the pit, circle, and cross again. There are papers in scientific journals by observers of the Beqa firewalkers, but no credible explanation has been found.

The Fijians were converted to Christianity by Methodist missionaries in the mid-nineteenth century. This happened at the same time as white traders were bringing to the islands the superior manufactured goods of Europe, and no doubt the god of the white men was given the credit for the steel axes and guns. So Methodism was accepted by the chiefs and followed by the commoners. It involved obvious changes in behaviour: no more cannibalism; only one wife at a time; bare breasts taboo; female bodies covered from shoulder to ankle by 'Mother Hubbard' dresses; and, later, no alcohol.

I think that the religious life of the Fijians developed slowly into two distinct areas: the ancient, inexplicable supernatural spirits of their ancestors, which never quite lost their *mana*, or power, and the moral code of the Christians. There was no stress on the supernatural in Christianity, just as there was no moral content to the traditional beliefs. By the time I lived among the Fijians, the practices of the past had been largely forgotten – though I did meet a man who had eaten a piece of the Revd Thomas Baker, the last victim of cannibalism, in 1867. To be Christian was to be civilized.

The moral code of Methodism in Fiji was that of the British lower middle-class, from which most of the missionaries came. Though the early ones drank alcohol, and some developed severe problems in the heat and loneliness, by the time I arrived Methodism was strictly teetotal. It involved regular attendance at church wearing uncomfortable clothes: coats and ties for the men and Mother Hubbards for the women; chastity before marriage and fidelity afterwards; no work and little play on Sundays; plenty of Bible reading and long and frequent choir practice. The singing was magnificent. Put any four Fijians together and you have a barbershop quartet; harmony seems as natural as eating. Every village builds, maintains and is proud of its church. And on Sundays they go there to sing. But the sermons, which are lengthy, have a tendency to dwell on the consequences of sin; the moral aberrations condemned range from adultery to weeding the garden on Sundays. Unsurprisingly, few of the expatriates are drawn to Methodism in Fiji.

The expatriate life in a small colony is testing. You find yourself posted to a country station with perhaps half a dozen other families all clustered together in the government compound. They are totally bored with each other. As a new arrival, you are immediately fêted, which means that you meet all the residents at once on one evening when everybody gets rather drunk and matey. The rest of that first week you meet the couples individually, being asked to dinner by each one, when they tell you how much they hate each other and how close they are to murder or suicide. After that first week you go into hiding for a while, pretending to be ill or to have a 'family crisis' – a generic term which is never explained and always accepted – and then you have to start the tedious but inevitable social round. Of course there are highlights: wonderful eccentrics who build ships from matchsticks, study Sanskrit, or play the bagpipes naked at midnight on the lawn; escapees from mysterious contexts back home with hints of aristocratic or artistically glamorous connections.

Expatriate colonial life has been well described in the rash of memoirs which appeared from retired colonial officers wedged into the depths of Dorset during the dissolution of the Empire. Though the British colonies were spread over most of the world map, conditions in the expatriate enclaves seem to have been the same. I described them in a notebook provided by the government of Fiji which I still have. (On the cover is a label with the words THIS COVER HAS BEEN IMPREGNATED WITH AN INSECTICIDAL SOLUTION. The words are only just legible because the label has been eaten by insects.) This is what I wrote about colonial society in 1957:

It is a very self-conscious group because it feels itself to be under observation. 'The natives,' say the old hands, 'are always watching you.' Since the natives are assumed to be *in statu pupillari*, they must never be allowed to see anything which might reduce their respect for their colonial masters. So the expatriate society tends to behave in public like the staff and governing body on the platform at school speech day. Dress and deportment are bound by social convention, but not those of contemporary England: we preserve here fashions long since discarded back home. And people endure agonies to be presentable. I know women have done this for centuries, but here a man will wear an impervious sharkskin dress shirt to dinner at Government House, so that the sweat can collect round his waist and not soak through and spoil the immaculate whiteness of his front.

As a defence against conversation I started to learn bridge. Silence, in company, is never boring; repetitive anecdote always is. I used to fantasize that people should be born with

one of those digital counters in the middle of their foreheads
like the ones which count down to the detonation of bombs
in James Bond films. Each would be set at birth with the
number of words a person could utter during a lifetime; when
the figures hit zero, the person would be struck dumb. Then
everybody would look in the mirror each morning and take
care not to use up words unnecessary in the course of the
day . . . But, alas, life was less well organized, and the people
I met seemed to need to talk the whole time we were together.
The only period of silence was when bent over cards in a
game of bridge.

The first Muslim I met was my court clerk, Wazid Ali Khan.
The immediate impression was of a man who had unusual
self-possession. He had a low wage and lived in a small house
in a dirty town, but his shirts were always spotless white and
his trousers neatly pressed. He was quietly unassertive, and
there was a certain reserve in his manner. I felt he was ruled
by certain unwavering proprieties, and thought at first it was
the influence of his job. The court clerk knows more about
court procedure than the magistrate, and is always on the
alert to correct a deviation that might result in a decision
being reversed on appeal. So, although he always sat below
the dais on which were my chair and table, and looked up at
me deferentially – never forgetting to preface his remarks
with a 'Your Honour' – we both knew that he was really in
charge.

All the rest of the staff were Hindu, and the contrast
between Wazid Ali and them was striking. After a few
months I realized that his sense of propriety was not a result
of his attachment to legal procedures but went deeper. It had
to do with his faith. Although he never directly spoke of this,
it was obvious that the spiritual dimension in his life was a
daily reality to which his actions were referred. And this was
something totally new to me. A faith which could be a central
reference point in a man's daily life, giving stability, self-

possession, consistency, without being assertive or aggressive, seemed worth investigation. I bought a copy of the Koran.

The first thing that struck me there was the view that the amassing of worldly possessions is displeasing to God. For this I felt an immediate sympathy: it echoed the texts I had so much enjoyed in Clifton Chapel, which had dire things to say about the rich. And then there was so much richly symbolic poetry in the Koran that stirred the imagination and aroused my curiosity: 'If My servants enquire of thee concerning Me,' God says to Muhammad, 'lo, I am near.' Indeed he is 'nearer to him than his own jugular vein'. And yet a man who would see the works of God should 'journey through the earth and see how He hath brought forth created beings'. In the journeying, 'Whithersoever ye turn, there is the Face of God.'

When I went on to discover that Islam recognizes the prophets of Judaism and Christianity, I felt immediately that it could be a reasonable successor to both. I agreed with its rejection of the idea that Christ was God, and its substitution of the notion that, like other prophets, he was a vehicle of the divine message to humanity seemed to me to fit in with the Christ of the New Testament. The Muslim objection to the Christian idea of Christ was simple: the divinity of the Son of God is nonsense. 'To be a son is less than divine, and to be divine is to be no one's son.'

Another feature of Islam which appealed to me was its tradition of scholarship. This was no simple primitive belief devised for the intellectually challenged but a faith which had inspired the creation of magnificent libraries and universities all over the world. These all promoted a culture which had religion at its heart, and this seemed to me more admirable than our own, in which religion had shrunk to what a small number of people do with a couple of hours on Sundays.

Islam contrasted favourably with Hinduism at my first country station. The Muslims there were law-abiding, family-oriented and generally rather more educated than the Hindus, who tended to be the cane farmers spread around the foothills. Whereas Islam proclaimed itself by the call to prayer from the mosque, Hinduism was represented by the weird animist paintings and statues which stood, flower-decked, by the side of the road, and by the annual spree of the Holi festival, when men and women dashed about the streets and showered each other with yellow ochre. I formed the impression that Islam was a faith more advanced, civilized, and therefore worthy of study.

At this time I was being guided in my approach to exotic faiths by the Pelican book entitled *Comparative Religion*, by A. C. Bouquet, a muscular Christian who is identified on the back cover as a sometime scholar of Trinity College, an army chaplain and 'President of the University Judo (Ju-jitsu) Club'. His comment was 'At its best Islam produces a dignified and restrained type of character, perhaps not unlike that of some Scotch Calvinist Christians. At its worst, it makes for a non-moral craftiness.' I rejected this view as being obviously narrow-minded and telling more about the prejudices of writer than about his subject. My rejection was later tempered by experience.

Before I had the chance to enrol myself as a serious student of Islam under the guidance of a local imam, I was posted to another country station where there were no Muslims and no mosque. Here I met a man with an astonishing combination of attributes: university degrees in philosophy and theology, a sensitive acute discerning intelligence, and a firm belief that God made the world.

Catholic priests were a bewildering novelty to me. As a child I had known of Catholics as the people who lived in big houses behind high walls. Their faith, I gathered, was something exotic and had to do with Italy. I remember that my mother had once told me if I had too much to do with them they might brainwash me into joining them, and that if they did they would 'blacken my dickie'. (This particular initiation ritual she associated with most societies apart from the Co-op, so I didn't take it seriously.) I have mentioned briefly noticing the existence of Catholics through their absence at church parades in the army, but, oddly, I had met nobody I knew to be Catholic since then.

The Catholic priests were amiable and disconcerting. They existed in defiance of what I had taken to be a natural law: education extinguishes superstition. These men were intelligent, even clever, widely read, with secular degrees and a robust attitude to life that included heavy drinking and telling smutty stories. They seemed completely down to earth and knew far more about politics (both local and international) and the way the world works than I did. And yet they believed they had the power to forgive sins and work miracles with their hands. I started out on a long search into the nature of Catholicism that was to last for thirty years.

I began by ordering books from the Vidal Library, the Catholic bookshop in Suva, and worked my way steadily through the series Faith and Fact, which was exactly to my taste because it was rationally compartmentalized into sections dealing with history, dogma, ritual, art, architecture, etc. Short books, some of them were masterpieces of condensation setting out the main bodies of knowledge subsumed under their titles.

The fundamental attitude of the Catholic Church towards its claim to authority I found very persuasive. If Christ had founded a Church against which 'the gates of hell shall not prevail', it was reasonable to suppose that this Church would still be in existence. But there was (as I then thought) only one Church which claimed to have been in existence since New Testament times, which had universal outreach, and which had refused to change its doctrines to keep up with the shifting fashions of human thought. It was perfectly clear to any reasonable person that the church founded by Christ could not be one of the Protestant ones, as these did not exist before the Reformation. I also felt I could reasonably reject Protestantism because it had exchanged the authority of tradition for that of the Bible, the inconsistencies and errors of which I had catalogued at Oxford. I remember enjoying at this time the story of the parishioner who went to his Catholic priest one day to admit that he had lost his faith.

'You've not –' said the priest, 'you've not become a Protestant?' The parishioner was indignant: 'Father,' he said reprovingly, 'it's my *faith* I've lost. Not my *reason*.'

The Catholic Church's claim to infallibility, which many people found hard to accept, seemed to me perfectly reasonable in that, if a deposit of the truth had been entrusted to a Church by a divine power, then surely that power would take steps to ensure that the deposit was kept unadulterated.

I was predisposed to admire Catholic theology because I had recently discovered the pleasures of reading law. I had to sit examinations in the subject to qualify for appointment as a magistrate. I expected to find the subject dull, the textbooks fussy and fusty, but was delighted to find that the ones I was encouraged to study were masterpieces of clarity and precision. Kelly's *Criminal Law*, Winfield's *Contract* and *Tort*, Maitland on legal history, Pollock on jurisprudence – I read them all with relish at being in contact with minds that were able to make such distinctions and differences with such elegance. Case law had all the variety and excitement of fiction with the added spice that it had all happened to real people. Criminal law categorized human behaviour with such exactitude, allotting to each aberration its appropriate penalty. It appealed to what I have come to regard as the least amiable aspect of my personality: a strong sense of justice.

When I turned to Roman Catholic books on moral theology I found the same admirable qualities of thoroughness and care in the punctilious grading of degrees of sinfulness. I enjoyed the subject as a hybrid between criminal law and etiquette, and spent some time and concentration on the sexual-aberration sections, which were always in Latin and which I used as a recipe book for new ideas for sensual pleasure to try out when the opportunity arose.

My preoccupation with moral theology gave rise to a short poem. Its genesis was in a fantasy I often had when travelling overseas and sleeping alone in hotel bedrooms. I would imagine myself drifting off to sleep when the door would gently open and a lithe and sinuous belly dancer with skin like satin would slide her well-oiled body beneath the sheets. In this situation, I asked my Catholic friends, would I be held morally responsible? Surely a person is guiltless if tempted beyond his power to resist? Their answer saddened me. God, they said, does not allow us to be tempted beyond our capacity to rebuff the tempter. And it occurred to me that, to be consistent, God, if there is a God, would not persuade us of his existence beyond our power to resist. I wrote a poem about this.

FREEDOM: *A Moral Theologian's Lament*

I have always aspired to be tempted
By a woman too strong for my will
So the pleasure that's in
That particular sin
Could be mine without paying the bill.

But God, you know, won't allow it.
You can look up the text in St Paul:
1 Corinthians 10
Verse 13 – says that men
Can resist, if they will, when they fall.

And the fact that we're guaranteed freedom
To choose between evil and good
Means it wouldn't be right
To tempt you one night
If you couldn't say 'No' when you should.

Now this seems to me rather depressing.
Is that what it means – to be free?
I'm unable to say
At the end of the day
'Someone else is to blame – it's not me!'

And this freedom is going to prevent me
Being forced into faith by a fix
From a God who supplies
In front of my eyes
Inexplicable conjuring tricks.

When the Pharisees asked, you remember,
To be shown some credentials divine,
They were kept in the dark
With a cutting remark
About people who ask for a sign.

But God used to be really persuasive:
Think of Moses, the Pharaoh, St Paul –
Just to mention a few –
After all they went through
Couldn't still believe nothing at all.

So why has he stopped burning bushes;
Turning rods into snakes, serving dinner;
And parting the sea
So his people could flee
But know they were backing the winner?

It's because the advancement of science
Cataloguing predictable things
Means that if there's a flaw
In the natural law
Then there must be a God pulling strings.

But a God pulling strings unmistakably *is*:
He exists – just as plain as a pot.
And in making his play
He has taken away
Our freedom to say that he's *not*.

The scholarship and the antiquity of the Catholic Church
were very appealing. I loved the language of the Latin Mass
(we were then pre-Vatican II), and had begun to brush up my

Latin after a fruitful encounter with a classics master on a ship. We were travelling out to Fiji on the leisurely six-week voyage of the *Southern Cross* via Australia when I met this man who mentioned that it was a pity that so many people, after a good grounding in Latin at school, never used the language again and allowed a skill that had been hard to acquire to atrophy. I was stirred by what he had to say, and decided that the easiest way to brush up my Latin would be to read a text I knew reasonably well. So when we put in at Perth I bought a copy of the New Testament in Latin and began to read it every morning on deck.

There was an immediate and almost magical side effect. I mention it now for the comfort of all travellers. I noticed that, for the first time on the voyage, I was left in peace to read. Nobody came up to ask if I would make a fourth at bridge or join a doubles at deck tennis. The fact that I had a small black book which was obviously a Bible in my hand made me unapproachable. Rather like a leper's bell. This was such a relief that, from that time, whenever I have had to travel by sea and there is a danger of being pressed into sociability, I simply carry and read a Bible (or hold a Bible with another book inside it) and I am left alone. It never fails.

But, apart from affording me a blessed relief from sociability on long sea voyages, the New Testament in Latin proved a pleasure. Because many of the passages were familiar, I could kid myself into believing I understood the Latin when I was just remembering the English. And there were passages, especially in John 14, which had the ring of poetry: *Non turbetur cor vestrum ... tanto tempore vobiscum sum ... Pacem relinquo vobis*. The pleasure of reading the Latin words was partly the fact that they had been around a very long time, and that the sounds they made had echoed in Christian churches for nearly two thousand years.

I began to read the *Summa Theologica* of St Thomas Aquinas, and was immediately bowled over by the breadth of his learning and the power of his intellect. Here was a man who, when setting out a proposition, first advances all the conceivable arguments against it before demolishing them and proving his point. How can you resist the persuasion of somebody who has anticipated and improved on your opposition? His methods of argument were rational and Aristotelian: he made no final appeal to the subjective and ineffable experiences into which so many Christians seemed to retreat. He did, of course, accept that revelation was a source of truth, but he also held that natural reason was an alternative route to the same truth.

The first Vatican Council had declared that the doctrine of the modern Catholic Church was consistent with his teaching:

> Our holy mother the Church holds and teaches that God, the first principle and last end of all things, can be known with certainty from the created world by the natural light of human reason.

As I had not been granted a revelation, I tried to follow the reasonable arguments of St Thomas to accept such truths as the existence of God and his creation of the world. He admits, at the beginning of the *Summa Theologica*, that the existence of God is not self-evident because 'no one can think the opposite of that which is self-evident . . . But the opposite of the proposition "God exists" can be thought . . . Therefore the proposition that God exists is not self-evident.' Aquinas's proofs of the existence of God are the famous five, to which I gave careful attention.

First the argument from motion: since everything that moves has been brought into being by something else, there must be at the beginning of the process an Unmoved Mover. This is God.

Second, the argument from efficient cause: there is a chain of cause and effect reaching back in time. The argument, like that of the Unmoved Mover, then goes on to claim that: 'the human mind cannot tolerate an infinite regression', so we have to postulate a First Cause, or Unmoved Mover at the beginning of the sequence. I found that my own mind was as uncomfortable with the postulate as the infinite regression, so I had to reject these proofs.

Third, the argument from possibility and necessity: since nothing that exists contains within itself the reason for its existence, there must be a sustaining force that keeps it in being. This seemed to me the most persuasive argument, though it told me nothing about the 'sustaining force' that would lead me to accept the Christian God.

Fourthly, the argument from gradation: things are considered more or less good, noble, true as they resemble that which is the maximum. God is that maximum. But a person can be fat or tall . . .

Fifthly, the argument from design: since the universe contains evidence that objects in it have a purpose, it is reasonable to suppose the existence of a designer. But Darwin had showed that accidental mutations coupled with environmental pressures could result in adaptations which looked as though they were pre-planned but were in fact simply there because the less suited had died out. So a credible alternative argument had been discovered in an age of science.

So, although the powerful mind of St Thomas Aquinas impressed me, I was not swept along by his arguments and began to read books by neo-Thomists who claimed that, although St Thomas had achieved the perfect synthesis of Christianity and philosophy, his medieval articulation of ideas had to be restated in modern terms to be accessible in the twentieth century. I found the neo-Thomists exciting as intellectual gymnasts and less easy to contradict, because their arguments were less clearly and unambiguously expressed. But I remained unconvinced.

I had found a more compassionate and human hero in John Henry Newman, whose *Apologia pro Vita Sua* I still think of as one of the world's great books. In it he writes, and I find these words today in my notebook:

A man may be annoyed that he cannot work out a

mathematical problem of which the answer is, or is not, given to him without doubting that it admits of an answer or that a particular answer is the true one. Of all points of faith, the being of a God is, to my own apprehension, encompassed with most difficulty and borne in upon our minds with most power.

It was a relief to find him admitting the difficulties; but I could not share with him the sense that the existence of God was borne in upon my mind at all.

Nor could I agree with the implications of the words that so much comforted Pascal in his struggles towards enlightenment: 'You would not be seeking me unless you had already found me.' I had certainly not 'found' God. I was examining the question of his existence ('seeking' I might have rejected as being too emotive and likely to conduce to self-deception) largely because so many people I found admirable had settled on a positive answer. It seemed to me that, if God did exist, and was at all interested in our attitude to him, the least he could do would be to permit the fact of his existence to be available to an unbiased and rational inquirer.

The theologians I read agreed that rational inquiry would take me along the right road, but not to the end of it. At that point, they agreed, I had to make the 'leap of faith'. This could be simply a psychological commitment to the unknowable, given impetus in the right direction by rational inquiry: a courageous acceptance of that for which proof is impossible. By following the investigations of the reason, I could amass what Newman called 'an assemblage of concurring and converging probabilities' pointing to revealed truth. And he went on to assert with his unfailing elegance 'that probabilities which did not reach to a logical certainty might create a mental certitude'.

Newman's approach appealed to my basically gradualist angle of attack on life. If the truth could be found by progressive approximation, then I could spend a lifetime amassing converging probabilities which would eventually compel me to a final deathbed confession – the only one which my Catholic friends assured me guaranteed an immediate entry to eternal bliss without so much as a stopover in Purgatory.

Sadly, my experience was that the probabilities did not converge. Every argument pointing to the existence of God was cancelled by a countervailing phenomenon: in nature we have the beauty of a snowdrop but we also have the ichneumon flies which deposit their eggs in the bodies of other insects; in human society we can produce Mother Theresa but we also throw up Adolf Eichmann. Voltaire's outraged reaction to the Lisbon earthquake when a benevolent and omnipotent God had caused, or at least permitted, the slaughter of forty thousand people was entirely reasonable. And don't we all agree with Ivan Karamazov's protest that if the edifice of human destiny has to include the undeserved suffering of one small child, we should give God back our ticket of admission?

The use of human reason as a path to religious truth was an exciting revelation to me at the time, since I had previously only come across rational arguments *against* religion. As a Humanist, I had accepted that all religion was irrational and appealed only to those who were prepared to sacrifice their reason to their emotions.

In Fiji I developed the habit of jotting down in a notebook ideas that came to me while shaving. Looking through them, I am surprised to find that, at this time when intellectual inquiry seemed to me the only road to knowledge, I wrote:

Scepticism, so common among intellectuals, is simply arrogance. Men need to feel that those fields in which they are competent are in some way superior to those in which they are not. So the scholar, who has received distinction through his intellect, needs to believe that the processes by which he has arrived at knowledge are superior to those of the unscholarly:

Peter France

> I am the Master of this College
> What I don't know isn't knowledge.

It would, after all, be unfair if the truth were to be revealed in some supra-rational way, without intellectual effort, to the unscholarly. So the intellectual needs to feel that the only road to knowledge is his road. The result is that he has to be sceptical about faith or revelation or mysticism for the sake of his self-respect: these roads to wisdom are uncomfortably democratic. The rationalist holds that those things which cannot be explained or conveyed in words from one person to another do not exist. But who can put into language the smell of a rose – or the experience of toothache – or of hearing great music – to somebody who has not had the experience for himself?

I cannot explain why, having written those words, they seem to have had so little effect on my spiritual progress. Looking back, I realize that I was constantly encountering situations from which I should have learned that reason has its limits and can even be perverse. One occurred shortly after I was posted to the capital, Suva, to work in the central-government offices there. It happened that a purge had been launched against homosexuals in the European community. A dour Scottish police superintendent was sent out to lead the campaign against criminal effeminacy, and he called at my house one day to ask for my help.

It was a Sunday morning. I had a weekly ritual on Sundays which involved sitting in the garden and reading. On this particular Sunday the sun was shining, and I responded by wearing only a floral *sulu*, or sarong, around my waist. I was suffering from a mild shaving rash, so I had powdered my face with prickly-heat powder. And, to complete the picture, being unable to find my sunglasses, I had borrowed my wife's, which had an attractive, swept-up style ornamented with gilt.

The superintendent was a trifle put out when, thus attired, I welcomed him with a cheery wave, but he recovered himself

74

enough to tell me that the book in the brown-paper parcel he was carrying was material evidence in his latest case and he needed my help. It had been found in the possession of a man accused of unnatural practices, and, since certain passages were marked, he thought they might provide a clue as to the exact nature of the practices in question. The book was in French, and he asked me to translate for him the marked passages. The book was *La Philosophie dans le boudoir* by the Marquis de Sade. It would be indelicate of me here to go into the details of the passages I translated. Suffice it to say that they related to certain activities involving riding-boots and a turkey. I was able to assure the superintendent that the only turkeys in Fiji were on the island of Taveuni, which the accused had never visited.

The incident is relevant here because of the message of the rest of the book. This was a carefully argued, highly intelligent and persuasive rational justification for the performance of activities which produced intense physical pleasure. Because Sade believed that the most intense pleasures issue from revulsions that have been overcome, many of these activities involved violence, torture, nauseating substances, wallowing in the unspeakable. And yet these were not the insane illiterate outpourings of a savage but the carefully reasoned arguments of a highly educated French aristocrat. I found the writings of de Sade to be the *reductio ad absurdum* of the philosophy which holds that the human reason has sovereignty in the moral sphere.

It was in Fiji that I also first came across the writings of C. S. Lewis. I had met the man himself at my viva-voce examination after finals at Oxford, where he gently chided me for misspelling Lady Mary Wortley Montagu – beauty, wit and toast of the Kit-Cat Club. (I've just looked her up again, to be sure.) I had read his famous books of literary criticism but did not enjoy them as he had an enthusiasm for allegory which I could not share. I remember hearing at Oxford something about his having 'got religion' in his dotage – it being particularly scandalous that a scholar of his eminence should have plumped for an evangelical form of Christianity. But I had read none of his religious books, which were neither part of the syllabus nor in my sphere of interest at the time.

The first of his books I read in Fiji was *The Screwtape Letters*, which is a delight to both believer and unbeliever. I noted with some surprise these words in the introduction: 'There are two equal and opposite errors into which our race can fall about the devils. One is to disbelieve in their existence. The other is to believe, and to feel an excessive and unhealthy interest in them. They themselves are equally pleased by both errors and hail a materialist or a magician with the same delight.' Here was a grown man, an intellectual who held a senior academic position at the greatest university in the world, apparently holding that 'devils' did exist. But then he wrote so much imaginative fiction that I decided he must be playing games.

He was a brilliantly entertaining writer, and I grabbed a copy of *Surprised by Joy* – the account of his conversion – soon after it came out in 1955. But it was a disappointment. I looked for an intellectually comprehensible account of how he, an undeniably sharp and perceptive mind, could have come to accept the improbabilities of Christianity, but all I found was that he had got into the top deck of a bus going up Headington Hill an unbeliever and had got off the bus a Christian. Some internal transformation had taken place which he found totally authoritative and I found completely unconvincing.

But the greatest interest for me in the book was his rather special use of the word 'joy', which had so upset me when Ada Hopper used it in Clifton Chapel. He uses the word in the sense of 'an unsatisfied desire which is itself more desirable than any satisfaction'. This seems, on the face of it, to be complete nonsense, but, because of the quality of mind of the man penning the words, it deserves to be paused over. He goes on to write that joy, in his sense, is to be sharply distinguished from happiness and from pleasure. 'Joy (in my sense) has one characteristic and one only in common with them: the fact that anyone who has experienced it will want it again.' This had been my reaction to seeing the Leonardo painting in Paris, to hearing the prelude to *The Mastersingers* in Huddersfield Town Hall. But though I had later heard the prelude many times on record and in concerts, and always expected the same sudden thrill that had hit me on that first occasion, it never came. And Lewis goes on to comment that, though we may long for joy more than for all the pleasures in the world, 'Joy is never in our power and pleasure often is.'

He goes on, 'Only when your whole attention and desire are fixed on something else . . . does the "thrill" arise. It is a by-product. Its very existence presupposes that you desire not it but something other and outer.' You can't make it happen. And if it does start to happen and, through introspection, you examine what is happening – to enjoy it more – it fades. I remember a radio talk given by Rabbi Lionel Blue in which he spoke of the Holy Spirit as a tiny bird which occasionally and unexpectedly would land on your shoulder and fill you with inspiration; but if you turned your head to look at it it would fly away.

Lewis came to the final conclusion that his error lay in thinking that what he wanted was joy in itself and not the object. 'Joy itself, considered simply as an event in my own mind, turned out to be of no value at all. All the value lay in that of which Joy was the desiring.'

I copied those words into a notebook at the time, and later added a couple of relevant quotations. The first was from Henri Bergson's *L'Énergie spirituel*:

La Nature nous avertit par un signe précis que notre destination est atteinte. Ce signe est la joie. Je dis la joie, je ne dis pas la plaisir . . . La plaisir n'indique pas la direction où la vie est lancée. Mais la joie annonce toujours que la vie a réussie . . .

And the second was from *My Dear Timothy*, the autobiography of Victor Gollancz:

> In pleasure and happiness as such ... there is always a specific accent on the self ... If you feel happy at the beauty of a Spring day the essence of the matter is that *you* are feeling happy ... Joy, on the other hand, is not yours. It is something that happens, some potential that is realized when you and Reality are at one; and happens not in you but in Reality, or happens, rather, only in you because it happens in Reality and you and Reality are one.

I was beginning to feel that Ada Hopper was a more profound person than I had realized.

In early 1966 I was posted to the district of Ba on the main island of Viti Levu. There I met a man who deepened my awareness of spiritual matters. He would giggle with disbelief if he read that. He was an Indian, from India – that is, not born in Fiji – and his name was S. B. Patel. He was about five feet tall, with a high domed forehead and a shock of white hair that made him look like a sun-tanned Bertrand Russell. The comparison would have pleased him as he was a Russell fan. S. B., as he was known, was a solicitor in the township of Lautoka, about twenty miles from my house in Ba. He drove a large black Humber Hawk, and to see him approach along the narrow roads of the town was unnerving because the car appeared driverless. S. B. could only just see over the dashboard, and used to peer through the steering wheel to find his way.

He was well known in the colony and a suspicious figure to the police Special Branch because rumour had it that he had been sent to Fiji from India on a subversive mission. He had been private secretary to Gandhi and so was involved for a time in the independence movement in India. It was said that he was secretly organizing the Indians in Fiji against their colonial masters, though quite what he was organizing them to do was never clear. I liked him immediately, because he looked like Bertrand Russell, had no respect for the respectable, and had a house full of books.

He used to ask me to tea occasionally and we would sit in his large garden – he always on a canvas swing seat and I on a chair – and talk. For a time, I asked him about problems connected with my work: my new district was mainly Indian, and my years in Fiji had mainly been spent with Fijians, so I was in need of guidance. He always delighted me by telling me to ignore instructions, even from the most exalted personages of the colonial administration: 'Don't listen to him. The man's an idiot. Always was.' He would tell me who, of the local people, I could trust and who were the villains. But, above all, he gave me a sense of proportion – much needed when I was trying to cope with a strike by cane farmers or embezzlement on the town council.

Whenever I went to him in a state of pother about some piece of local chicanery he would talk to me about Gandhi and the patient way he handled the British. We would try to work out how he had found the strength to be so long-suffering and the wisdom to be so often right. And how – this I felt constantly applied to my situation – he had managed to cope with knowing that he was right when those in charge of events were wrong. S. B. would lend me books, often by or about Gandhi, and he would intrigue me about Hinduism by odd remarks and quotations. One, from Radhakrishnan, I copied into my commonplace book of the time:

> Hinduism is wholly free from the strange obsession of the Semitic faiths that the acceptance of a particular religious metaphysic is necessary for salvation, and non-acceptance thereof is a heinous sin meriting eternal punishment in hell.

When I told S. B. that his revelations about Hinduism, which I had previously thought a poor enough thing, attracted me, he gave me a marvellous little book by Chakravarti Rajagopalachari. I was delighted to find that the author had been a considerable scholar – he had published books on my old hero Marcus Aurelius and the Vedanta, as well as editions of the *Mahabharata* and the *Ramayana*. He had been a close associate of Gandhi, and wrote, 'The greatness of Gandhiji and the strength of his movement were entirely derived from and rooted in Vedanta.'

After thirty years, during which time I have read many books and interviewed many people about Hinduism, it is difficult to remember what first impressed me about it. I think it may have been the claim that Vedanta, which is what Rajagopalachari calls the religion of the Hindus, not only is the oldest faith but also anticipated the basic theories of biology and physics. The sovereignty of God is exercised through the laws of nature, and the universe is the result of the gradual unfolding of creative power.

Or perhaps it was the doctrine of *karma*, which appealed to my rigid sense of justice. I was never entirely comfortable with the Roman Catholic practice of confession, which in certain circumstances seemed to wipe out the consequences of human acts. Vedanta holds that the law of cause and effect is unalterable and applies to all human activities. This means that it is foolish to do something and then hope to undo it because its effects are not to our liking. No act can ever fail to produce its result. The effect lies inherent in the cause, just as the tree lies potentially encased in the seed. This is not a doctrine of fatalism, because we are free to choose the acts we perform: we must not expect to avoid or be able to obliterate their consequences.

This admirable pragmatism was set in a view of reality I found familiar but unconvincing. This is that the world as we know it is only the symbol of a more real, eternal and spiritual world. The world as it presents itself to our senses is *maya*, an illusion, whereas true reality is inaccessible to the senses. Here I found myself siding with Dr Johnson, who, when told about the subjective idealism of Bishop Berkeley, simply kicked a large stone so that his foot rebounded from it and said, 'Thus I refute him.' (I only later came to realize that the illusion does not refer to the objective world of the senses itself, but to the human view that this world is the only reality.)

I found very appealing the idea that we each of us, as humans, have a touch of divinity within: 'It is the inner light, the concealed witness, that which endures and is imperishable from birth to birth,' writes Radhakrishnan in his edition of the Bhagavadgita. This would explain the little bit of me that responds to music and poetry, the bit that rejoices in Sir Thomas Browne's words 'there is something in us that can be without us and will be after us' – and in his claim, which echoes precisely the teaching of the Vedanta, 'There is surely a piece of divinity in us, something that was before the elements, and owes no homage unto the sun.'

But the most important revelation to me in Rajagopala-chari's book was one which called in question the value of the intellectual search for religious truth on which I had been engaged for so long – a search encouraged and sustained by the scholastics. He suggests that intelligence, scholarship and application are not enough:

> A wall or a hill or a tree is visible to saint and sinner alike. The truth in a proposition of geometry can be seen by everyone alike whether he be a good man or a wicked . . . Faults of character cannot affect the perception of a fact. If the soul exists, it should be possible to ratiocinate and arrive at a clear conclusion. Why should character be a condition prerequisite for knowledge of any kind?

The answer to this question constitutes, for Rajagopalachari, by far the most important part of Vedanta:

> The soul is not a material limb or organ of the body. It is not located in any particular part of the body. It permeates body and mind. Unless the mind is clear, that which permeates it will not assume a distinct form or become known. It is one thing to see external objects, but it is altogether a different process to perceive an entity which is hidden in our own inner

being and whose imperceptibility is due to our own passions . . . It is not intellectual ignorance that blinds our vision
but desires and attachments.

The idea that cognition may have a moral content, that
realities perceptible to a good person may be invisible to a
bad one, irrespective of intelligence, recalls, of course, the
teachings of Jesus about the kingdom of heaven and little
children. When I first saw it formulated in this way, as a
proposition advanced by a serious thinker rather than the
pious hope of a Sunday-school teacher, it gave me pause; but
I dismissed the idea as one of the myths put about by
religious people to encourage good behaviour.

Certainly its truth would have excluded me from spiritual
advancement. I was working my way through libraries of
books written by serious-minded religious people but was
concentrating the rest of my energies on fleshly delights.
Religion was intriguing but still remote, and I found in those
days that, in times of real stress, a cigarette was far more use
than the four Gospels. Life was full and exciting because
there was plenty of food and drink and sex in it. The
intellectual pleasures of theology and philosophy were a
relaxation during the intervals, but, given the choice by my
fairy godmother, I should have preferred to spend a couple of
hours working out with a nymphomaniac contortionist
rather than in conversation with Cardinal Newman.

It has become notorious that the expatriate community in a
tropical colony busies itself by working through the gamut of
the lively sins. Drink is plentiful and cheap; servants increase
the leisure hours: 'What men call gallantry and gods adultery/
Is much more common where the climate's sultry.' This was
particularly so during the Swinging Sixties. I was an eager
recruit to the exotic ethos, and spent so much time and
energy on such a variety of excesses that a Catholic friend of
mine one day advised me, should I ever be converted, my first
confession should be of only three words: 'Father, the lot.'

Chapter Four

I left Fiji when democracy arrived. What Churchill called the worst form of government apart from all the other forms that have been tried, was the goal of independent nations; or perhaps it would be nearer the truth to say that it was the only form of government to which the British felt they could hand over with international approval. It seemed to me that in Fiji it was a bad idea.

In 1874 the chiefs of Fiji had handed over their country to Queen Victoria and her descendants, who were neither empowered nor expected to hand on the country to anybody else. But in 1970, when independence came, there were more Indians than Fijians in the country, so that a system which aimed at the eventual evolution of a parliamentary democracy, albeit with safeguards for the Fijian people, seemed likely to result in an eventual Indian takeover.

My job at the time was Permanent Secretary in the Ministry of Fijian Affairs, which meant that I was responsible to the government for the conduct of that department and, worse, held responsible by Fijians for the conduct of the government. I had spent fifteen years travelling around the islands, accepting the hospitality and respect of the people, who decked their houses with photographs of the royal family and knew that the British would never let them down. I had a photocopy of the Deed of Cession under plate glass on my desk, so that all decisions I took, the advice I gave, the letters I signed were in its presence. When the arrangements were finally made which, it seemed to me, violated its provisions, I did not have the courage to stay. So I left.

I had never planned to leave Fiji permanently. I could think of nowhere else I wanted to be. Fortunately, I was taken into a situation which, had I been given control of the blueprints for my ideal life, I should have designed for myself: The Institute of Advanced Studies at the Australian National University.

In 1970 the academic world as now was terrorized by a university policy known as 'publish or perish'. This meant that if you had an academic job you could hold on to it only if you regularly published material in academic journals. This was, of course, good for the journals, who were amply supplied with pabulum, but not for their readers, who were frequently bombarded with trivia. The Australian National University set up its Institute of Advanced Studies in defiance of this policy. It gathered together scholars from all over the world into a centre of sylvan calm at Canberra where, walking among cool green lawns and plashing fountains, they could, like the peripatetic philosophers of the Periclean age, exchange deep thoughts and give birth to great ones. In practical terms, if you had tenure there you could live on a generous salary in idyllic surroundings with access to ample libraries.

So, when I was offered a research fellowship at the Institute (I had completed a PhD there in 1966, on leave of absence from Fiji), I knew life could hold nothing better. At last, freed from pressures and responsibilities, I should be able to devote myself to reading and to the amiable companionship of scholars more intelligent and better equipped than I to probe life's mysteries. The anxieties of reconciling the irreconcilable were past; ahead lay a golden time of gently growing wiser.

I learned one important lesson at Canberra. Most people know it from the age of about twelve, but I was a slow developer: brains aren't everything. I had assumed that if you choose a small group of particularly intelligent people and place them in ideal surroundings, with a secure job and a generous salary, you would inevitably create a blissful community. But this, I discovered, is not true. At Canberra, there was as much neurosis, backbiting, petty jealousy and infantile aggression as in any community of academics anywhere. My colleagues, I soon realized, were indeed very clever; but they were not clever enough to be happy.

So I left Canberra with my confidence in the supremacy of the intellect having suffered another dent. I had a small pension from Fiji and hoped to supplement it somehow back in England. I was too old to start off at the bottom of the ladder in theatre, but thought that broadcasting might be a less aggressive, more sedentary form of theatre for which I might have retained some residual talent. I auditioned at the BBC studios in Bristol, and was given odd jobs doing interviews for *Woman's Hour* and reading the letters in *Any Answers*. Eventually I discovered an unusual talent which led to a career in broadcasting and an insight into a world which became highly relevant to my spiritual journey.

The talent was a complete inability to retain in my memory any facts relating to natural history. I had noticed that during the torture of school 'nature walks', when we boys had to suffer the humiliation of walking along country lanes in a double crocodile file holding the sticky hands of little girls, I could never remember the names of the flowers, no matter how often I heard them. By the age of eighteen I could tell a dandelion from a daisy and even identify a robin if it was close at hand and looking me straight in the eyes, but that was the extent of my knowledge of the world about us. I was enthusiastic about it, but totally, and it seemed irredeemably, uninformed.

When one of the radio producers of the BBC's Natural History Unit, based in Bristol, discovered this unusual combination of enthusiasm and invincible ignorance, she offered me a job presenting a weekly radio programme called *The Living World*. I was taken out into the countryside by an expert in some feature of the natural world – birds, bees, bats, foxes or fleas – and we would search for, discover, and then discuss the week's topic on the spot, with the creature under our eyes and often in our hands. The integrity of the programme was inviolable, so that one night, after we had spent six hours trudging through the New Forest in a fruitless search for glow-worms, the producer refused to allow our expert to pop under a bush a couple he had brought along in a matchbox and pretend to find them.

These expeditions were always exciting and stimulating to me – though never really educational, because of the above-mentioned inability to remember anything. This did, however, allow me to react with genuine surprise and enthusiasm to things I had heard several times before, and the expressions of amazement stimulated listeners and kept me in the programme.

But I made one astonishing discovery which stayed with me and was fed by the weekly sessions with natural scientists: these were adult and highly educated men and women who seemed to be in every other respect totally normal; but they really believed that humanity had evolved accidentally over a long period of years from green slime.

In fact I came to realize that a revolution had happened in academic circles. Until the University Tests Act of 1871, no scholar had been able to take up an academic post at one of the older universities unless he declared his belief that God had made the world; now, it seemed, nobody could get an academic job in the natural sciences unless he or she was ready to stand up and deny this. Biological determinism ruled. There was a certain logic in this: the received wisdom in the biological sciences was that humans were divided into Evolutionists and Creationists. Evolutionists accepted the theory, first elaborated by Charles Darwin, that animals had evolved over millions of years through 'numerous, successive, slight modifications'; Creationists (according to the Evolutionists) accepted the biblical account that God, who had a long white beard and lived in the sky, had created animals in all their diversity on the fifth and sixth days. The best way to sell a highly implausible theory is to insist that the only alternative is even less plausible. The ones who came in on Darwin's side got the academic jobs.

In our field trips this change of commitment was always evident. Whereas a ramble around the English countryside with the Revd Gilbert White would have involved his constant refrain that the song of the nightingale or the wings of the butterfly were a celebration of the glory of God, our experts explained that these were simply adaptive mechanisms which increased the chances of gene survival.

When discussing with biologists the credibility of the theory which underpinned their work, I was struck by the intensity of their attachment to it. It was as if the nineteenth-century battle between biblical fundamentalism and the Darwinists was being refought. But the religious fervour was, strangely, on the side of the biologists. If I raised objections, they would often react as if I was not completely sane or had insulted their fundamental creed – the sacrosanct principles according to which they lived and moved and had their being.

And, out of the plenitude of my ignorance, I did have objections. These highly educated scientists held that random genetic mutations caused physical changes which gave certain animals an advantage over others in the struggle to survive and reproduce. These physical changes, gradually evolving over millions of years, had resulted in animals being the shape they are. So birds had evolved from reptiles by gradually developing, through 'numerous, successive, slight modifications', wings. But, it seemed to me, an undeveloped wing, a mere stump on the back, would be not a help but a hindrance to survival. It would certainly make either hunting or running away more difficult. So unless wings capable of sustaining flight had suddenly appeared in one mutation – which nobody suggested – they could not, by a process of natural selection, have developed at all.

Such objections are well known and have been often rehearsed by now. The eye, which Darwin admitted gave him a cold shudder, could hardly have evolved because a light-sensitive patch on the cheek of some primitive animal gave it a survival advantage over its competitors. There are indeed 'eyes' of increasing complexity through limpets, squid, snails and jellyfish; but to arrange these different species in order of complexity and suggest that they indicate a process of evolution is, as somebody said, rather like placing a candle, a torch and a searchlight side by side and assuming a genealogical relationship. And how many of the accidental changes would have had to appear simultaneously to give an evolutionary advantage? These questions are still being raised among the experts, and I had certainly no right to an opinion on the many complexities of the subject. But, overall, it seemed to me in my most rationalist and materialist phase that the theory of the evolution of species by the sole agency of the influence of natural selection on random mutations did not have an edge in credibility over the old man with the white beard in the sky.

The mid-1960s was a time when animal behaviourists took over from depth psychologists as the experts who tell us why we behave as we do. Robert Ardrey's *The Territorial Imperative* explained that we are aggressive because we are descended from a particularly bad-tempered carnivorous hominid which hunted to extinction its more gentle vegetarian relative. In contrast, Konrad Lorenz in *On Aggression*, published the same year, explained that humans are homicidal because they are descended from vegetarian hominids who, lacking the dental equipment to kill each other, never developed the behavioural avoidance of mortal combat that prevented the carnivores from wiping each other out. You could take your choice on the mutually exclusive explanations, but both located urges to aggression deep in the unalterable past of the human race so we were able to feel less guilty about our bad behaviour. Then came Desmond Morris with the best-selling *The Naked Ape*, which in racy prose revealed to the world of 1967 that our basic behavioural traits are held in common with our cousins the apes, and so to act like monkeys is to act naturally. This message accorded well with the spirit of the times.

I think now that the work I did in natural history, although superficial and hampered by the memory defect I've mentioned, did something to undermine the reliance on the authority of science which I was cultivating as a Humanist. When the theories of the animal behaviourists blossomed into the new science of sociobiology, I was finally disillusioned. The sociobiologists claimed that all human behaviour was coded in our genes and moulded by natural selection. They analysed human nature, and saw in it the products of the struggle for survival. So humans are aggressive, self-aggrandizing, territorial, selfish animals genetically programmed to maximize their reproductive fitness. When they lapse into altruism, this can be explained by an expectation of reciprocal reward or, in extreme cases, the sacrifice of an individual to increase the chances of survival of the genetic pool to which he belongs.

The mental gymnastics necessary to preserve this attitude are remarkable, and occasionally fun. Explanations of sexual behaviour have to be particularly nimble. Among animals generally, especially birds, the male is more brightly coloured and highly adorned. Among humans, outside Italy, the reverse is the norm. Why? Because, say the sociobiologists, women advertise their reproductive fitness by accentuating their large breasts and wide hips. (Sociobiologists clearly don't come across fashion magazines.) Male drabness shows a penny-pinching conservative nature that is likely to make a good provider; flashy dressers are likely to be promiscuous and run off.

The story of spinach is another highlight of sociobiological reasoning. Children hate spinach and adults love it. This is because the oxalic acid which spinach contains prevents the absorption of calcium. Children have growing bones and need calcium; adults bones do not. So any gene which makes children dislike spinach and adults like it would be selected for. Sociobiology, which uses scientific method and scientific language to arrive at and promulgate conclusions which seem to me simplistic, was a great spiritual help to me in dislodging the confidence in scientific materialism I had grown to accept. My scepticism about the sceptics was fed by a remark from one of my Humanist heroes, J. B. S. Haldane, to the effect that humans could never become angels because we lack the genetic variation for wings and for moral perfection.

It was about this time that I came across a revealing quotation from Darwin which our biologists seemed to have overlooked:

> Up to the age of thirty or beyond it, poetry of many kinds . . . gave me great pleasure, and even as a schoolboy I took intense delight in Shakespeare, especially in the historical plays. I have also said that pictures gave me considerable and music very great delight. But now for many years I cannot endure to read a line of poetry: I have tried lately to read Shakespeare and found it so intolerably dull that it nauseated me. I have also lost almost any taste for pictures or music . . . My mind seems to have become a kind of machine for grinding general laws out of large collections of fact, but why that should have caused the atrophy of that part of the brain alone on which the higher tastes depend, I cannot conceive . . . The loss of these tastes is a loss of happiness and may possibly be injurious to the intellect and more probably to the moral character by enfeebling the emotional part of our nature.

I never quite had the courage to inquire of one of our reductionist biologists whether he agreed with his founding father that the pursuit of their craft was destructive of the higher sensitivities or undermining to the intellect and moral character.

It was while researching Darwinism that I first came across one of those unforgettable personalities that leave a lifelong impression: Darwin's cousin Francis Galton. His was one of the most powerful and wide-ranging intellects of the nineteenth century, the last age of the polymath. I was so excited by him that I spent six months reading everything he had written and putting together a radio documentary about him.

Galton was trained in medicine and mathematics. As a student, he had tried to work his way through the pharmacopoeia trying out the drugs on himself, in alphabetical order, the better to know their likely effect on his patients. He left off at croton oil, having established empirically that it is indeed, as the books claimed, effective violently and simultaneously as a purgative and an emetic.

Having completed his studies at Trinity College, Cambridge, Galton abandoned his idea of becoming a doctor and set out to explore the Sudan. He then published his book *Art of Travel* before turning to meteorology, in which he was the first to attempt to chart the weather on a large scale and to identify the anticyclone. In psychology, he pioneered the word-association tests which so impressed Jung. He started the system of using fingerprints to identify criminals, and attempted to establish by photography the existence of facial characteristics which indicate personality traits.

His interest in religion was anthropological, and, as an empiricist, he experimented on himself, to the extent of trying to gain an insight into the feelings of barbarians towards the power of human images they know to be of human handiwork. He tested himself by picking an object which in itself was unlikely to arouse feelings of devotion and then trying to invest it with divinity. He chose a comic picture of Punch:

> I addressed it with much quasi-reverence as possessing a mighty power to reward or punish the behaviour of men towards it and found little difficulty in ignoring the impossibility of what I professed. The experiment gradually succeeded; I began to feel, and long retained for the picture a large share of the feelings that a barbarian retains towards his idols, and learned to appreciate the enormous potency they might have over him.

But Galton's lifelong passion was for counting. If any

action or phenomenon was divisible into countable units, this was, for Galton, its most compelling aspect. Statistics were to him the key to the understanding of what he called the Science of Man. So he used statistics to calculate the intensity of boredom in a captive audience by calculating the 'Measure of Fidget', the relationship between the amplitude and the period of physical movement indicating the degree to which attention was caught; he worked out a 'Beauty Map' of the British Isles by pricking a piece of paper in his pocket every time he passed a pretty girl; he worked out a system of calculating which of his dinner guests had an 'inclination' to another by concealing pressure gauges under the legs of their chairs and recording the side on which their body weight inclined.

But the studies which most impressed me were those published in the *Fortnightly Review* under the title 'Statistical Enquiries into the Efficacy of Prayer'. Galton was at pains to point out that he was not seeking to throw light on how far it it is possible for a man to commune in his heart with his god. There were, he admitted, aspects of prayer which are private, personal and inaccessible to statistical inquiry. But there remain those specific requests for tangible benefits which are publicly made as part of the Church's ritual: their effects can be numbered among the countables of life.

He quoted views on prayer from leading authorities of his day, so as to be quite clear on what he was investigating. Smith's *Dictionary of the Bible* said of prayer, 'Its real objective efficiency . . . is both implied and expressed [in Scripture] in the plainest terms . . . We are encouraged to ask special blessings, both spiritual and temporal, in the hope that thus and thus only we may obtain them.' And Dr Hook, in his *Church Dictionary* stated, 'the general providence of God acts through what are called the laws of nature. By particular providence God interferes with those laws and He has promised to interfere on behalf of those who pray in the name of Jesus.'

Galton studied situations in which the same object was

pursued by classes similar in their physical but opposite in their spiritual states. Do those who pray, he asked, attain their objects more frequently than those who do not pray? As a medical man, he looked first at the influence of prayer on recovery from disease. Although he scoured the leading medical works of modern Europe which recorded the progress and therapeutic agencies relating to every known disease, he could find no reference to the therapeutic effect of prayer:

> In all countries and in all creeds, the priests urge the patient to pray for his own recovery and the patients' friends to help with their prayers. But the medical men, who are ever alert for the sanitary value of every influence, are silent on the subject of prayer.

He discovered that missionary voyages to unhealthy and barbarous regions were not attended by fewer mishaps than those of secular traders. Missionaries appear to have been carried off by storm, tropical disease or cannibals at about the same rate as slave traders. Pursuing his inquiries, Galton was unable to discover that businesses which had devout men on their boards prospered more than those which did not. And the universal presence of lightning conductors on churches seemed to indicate a lack of confidence in the providential care of the Almighty.

He considered the statistics kept by life-insurance offices, to establish whether prayerful habits had an effect on longevity, pointing out that from a business point of view it would be unwise to allow the devout, supposing their greater longevity even probable, to obtain annuities at the same rates as the profane. Before insurance offices accept a life, they make the most careful inquiries into the antecedents of the applicants but never ask whether prayer is part of their regular practice: 'Insurance offices, so wakeful to sanitary influences, absolutely ignore prayer as one of them.'

Galton went on to make his own statistical investigations

into the longevity of the devout by examining the lifespans of those members of the clergy who found their way into the standard biographical dictionaries alongside less prayerful classes. He was surprised to discover that, of the three classes of clergy, lawyers and medical men, the clergy were the shortest lived. 'Hence the prayers of the clergy for protection against the perils and dangers of the night, for protection during the day and for recovery in sickness appear to be futile in result.'

Even more suggestive were the statistics of life expectancy among members of the royal family, for whose health and protection daily petitions were offered. He discovered that sovereigns are literally the shortest lived of all who have the advantage of affluence. 'The prayer has, therefore, no efficacy unless the very questionable hypothesis be raised that the conditions of royal life may be naturally yet more fatal, and that their influence is partly, though incompletely, neutralized by the effects of public prayers.'

Galton's paper drew the fire of the *Spectator* on publication in 1872, and was dropped from collections of his writings. I found it massively entertaining and containing questions to which no satisfactory answer has yet been found. It put into my mind an idea which was never accepted for a radio programme but which I felt would be stimulating and sensational: The Bishop as Lunatic.

It seemed a good idea at the time. All the elements were there: personalities, conflict and more than a whiff of scandal. The programme could be recorded in a couple of hours in a studio and involved only three people: myself as chairman, a psychiatrist, and a bishop. The psychiatrist would examine the bishop professionally – that is, using his skill and judgement as a scientist of human psychology, unprejudiced by social or religious convention, to discover whether or not he was legally sane.

The law has always taken an interest in mental disorders, partly because of their relevance to the responsibility for criminal acts and partly because of the effect they have on the capacity of an individual to enter into binding contracts. So legal instruments from the earliest times distinguished between *idiots*, who were natural fools, incurable and with a disability they were born with, and *lunatics*, who became insane after birth and whose incapacity was, or might be, temporary or intermittent. Lunacy seemed to be the best bet for the bishop.

The Mental Health Act of 1959 dealt with mental disorders in the terms of its title: as illnesses. The symptoms of these illnesses were acts which were 'intrinsically irrational'. The Act defined mental disorder as 'arrested or incomplete development of mind'. Where the evidence for mental disorder was the nature of an act, that act had to be intrinsically irrational if it was to afford any presumption of the insanity of the doer. And the law held that the general rules and habits of a person alleged to be mentally disordered were of more weight in considering his sanity than particular acts done by him, however strange in themselves. So, although it would be colourful to produce in evidence an eccentric bishop's habit of occasionally boiling his watch and gazing at the egg, it would not be strictly relevant. To arrive at a safe diagnosis of mental disorder we would need evidence that the bishop regularly participated in activities which were 'intrinsically irrational' – or, in other words, not guided by reason.

Fortunately the general rules and habits of bishops tend to be regular, at least in theory, since they are governed by a liturgical framework imposed by the Church. But they are hardly those of a rational man. At morning prayer each day a bishop, together with his flock, must get on his knees and publicly confess that he has offended against holy laws and done those things he ought not to have done and that there is no health in him. On each occasion he receives absolution, so long as he truly repents and unfeignedly believes the holy Gospel, and he then goes on to pray that the rest of his life may be pure and holy. Yet the very same day, at evening prayer, he's back on his knees again, confessing himself a miserable offender and asking yet again for pardon. This can go on for years, and seems hardly compatible with rational behaviour.

If the bishop insists that he leads a life of such bustling and energetic immorality that each day between morning and evening prayer he manages to cram in enough offences against holy law to justify his repeated protestations of depravity, let us, following Francis Galton, turn to the Queen. The Book of Common Prayer records the following daily supplication for Her Majesty: 'Endue her plenteously with heavenly gifts; grant her in health and wealth long to live.' It is perfectly fair to ask the bishop what he thinks the effect of this prayer might be on Her Majesty's physical well-being and capital reserves. If he claims that both are improved by public prayer, then it can be pointed out that her father, George VI, died at the age of fifty-six, her uncle, Edward VIII, for whom we sang 'long to reign over us', did so for only ten months, and her grandfather, George V, equally the object of daily prayer, managed only the biblical three score years and ten. Edward VII died two years short of that.

Now, if the bishop daily performs acts which appear designed to produce a particular result and those acts can be shown to be wholly without effect, then he is not 'governed by reason', which would step in and stop him. Most of us learn, as children, that the little rituals we go in for to bring us luck – like not stepping on pavement cracks and crossing our fingers – don't seem to work, so we give them up. We may carry on making insignificant little half-conscious gestures, like not walking under ladders or tossing the spilt salt over our shoulders. Nobody could seriously be thought to be irrational because of them. But public petitionary prayer such as bishops go in for is a solemn act for which a particular place, costume and ritual are set aside. And it is performed deliberately, with full intellectual commitment. If it can be demonstrated to the reasonable man to be futile, what are we to think of the sanity of those who persist in it?

Further, we are taught by social anthropologists that the ceremonies of primitive people aimed at influencing the forces of nature – the sun, the moon and the weather – are indications of a pre-rational state of mind which civilized man has outgrown. Yet the Book of Common Prayer contains a petition for rain: 'Send us, we beseech thee, in this our necessity, such moderate rain and showers that we may receive the fruits of the earth . . .' And if the rain falls too abundantly on the earth the bishop may ask for fair weather, though in doing so he must admit that the rain was his fault in the first place: 'although we for our iniquities have worthily deserved a plague of rain and waters, yet upon our repentance . . . send us such weather as that we may receive the fruits of the earth . . .' Would not uttering such words in public with a conviction that they might affect the atmospheric conditions surely constitute, in the judgement of our psychiatrist, evidence of an unsound or at least an incompletely developed mind?

It was quite clear to me that, so long as the bishop held firm to the beliefs and practices of his faith, he would inevitably be certified insane, and this would bring the programme to a satisfactory end. Any bishop would do, since he could hardly deny the faith it was his duty to maintain. And as for the psychiatrist, so long as he applied the legal criteria rigorously, he would have to sign the certificate, though a thorough-going Freudian medical materialist might do the job with more flair.

The BBC steadily ignored the obvious potential of this idea and I was never able to arrange the confrontation. But my interest in religious subjects came to somebody's notice. By this time I had somehow managed to amass a personal library of over 5,000 books on different faiths, theology and Church history; I had flirted seriously with Islam, Hinduism, Buddhism and Roman Catholicism. My settled attitude was that religion was an engrossing field of study, not least because of the intriguing mystery of how so many intelligent people for so long should have practised self-deception so successfully. In the summer of 1974 I was given the chance to pursue this private interest professionally, by working in religious television.

Chapter Five

I began to work for BBC religious television at the dawn of a renaissance there. A new head of department had been appointed. He was Peter Armstrong – bright, young, thrusting, intelligent – and he introduced a revolutionary policy that transformed the ethos of the programme-makers and the quality of the output. His novel notion was that religious programmes should be watchable. They might even be arresting. In previous years these qualities had not been thought necessary in religious television, because of the existence of the 'God slot'.

The BBC had always preserved an aura of existing to improve the moral fibre of its customers. Furthering this end, since its inception it had regularly committed a certain amount of air time to religious programmes of a morally uplifting character. Since there were no other transmissions to listen to or watch while these were broadcast, these had been absorbed by a pliant nation without protest. But when the independent television companies began to compete, something clearly had to be done about religion. These companies were authorized to exist through renewable licences, and when the licences came up for renewal, they had to give the impression of something approaching seriousness of purpose. This involved putting out a small number of religious programmes. They began by making the same number as the BBC. Further – and this was crucial – they agreed to put out their religious programmes *at the same time*

99

as the BBC: for seventy minutes at prime time on Sundays. This was a gentleman's agreement between the broadcasters. It survived because everybody knew that the entire audience would switch over to the other channel if only one of them put out a religious programme. It made sense to have the 'God slot' at the same time, so that everybody would appear properly concerned and nobody would lose out.

At the BBC, religious programmes were left to the religious professionals: the clergy. They took the form of improving talks by parsons, or choir recitals in which the camera would pan slowly along lines of middle-aged ladies with their mouths open, all too often exempifying the dictum of H. L. Mencken that 'Christian endeavour is notoriously hard on female pulchritude.' These programmes had the single merit, in the eyes of the BBC's executives, of being cheap. Over on ITV the commercial people tackled the problem of religion in their usual way: by throwing money at it. Their choirs were radiantly dressed, swept by coloured spotlights, and showered with sequins; the sets were sumptuous, and the hymns were frequently led by pop stars.

The revolution which was launched in the BBC in 1974 called for the abandonment of the 'God slot' and the handing over of religious programmes from the religious to the television professionals. A small group of young men and women came together with the declared aim of making exciting, entertaining, well-crafted films on religious topics which, they felt, could move out of the protected slot into the bracing winds of competition with other programmes and still win an audience.

It worked. We began with a series called *Anno Domini*, which, renamed as *Everyman*, is still (in 1997) being regularly transmitted. We had a team of directors chosen for their skills at making films rather than their religious commitment, and their brief was simply to make good ones. The climate of the times encouraged experiment. Christianity in the West was split into contending factions: the supporters and opponents of Vatican II; liberation theology; the evangelical movement;

the feminists. Outside the mainstream churches many were searching for their own personal religious satisfaction in Eastern mysticism, encounter-group therapy, tyrannical sects and Messianic politics. It was a rich field for television documentaries.

My job on the team was that of writer/presenter. This involved researching, and sometimes coming up with, the initial idea; planning the approach, with the help of a researcher and director; then conducting the interviews on location, writing a script, and recording a voice-over. Often the film would include 'pieces to camera' in which I looked straight into the lens and said what I or the director, or preferably both of us, thought about what was going on. The work was exciting and varied, and could have enriched to the point of utterly confusing a personal religious quest, had I been on one. Fortunately, if I was, I didn't know it.

My position, the angle of attack from which I approached all projects, was that of the interested but impartial observer. It seemed to me that it should be possible to investigate religious experience rationally, just as it was possible to examine any other area of human experience and describe, analyse and interpret it in rational terms. The important thing was to be impartial and sympathetic. I was professionally uncommitted. When I left the series, after twelve years, they gave me a T-shirt with, printed on the chest, words I must have used a hundred times and which, unknown to me, had become my catchphrase: 'I AM JUST TRYING TO UNDERSTAND . . .'

The experiences of investigating and writing about different faiths, meeting and interviewing people intensely committed to them, was mind-expanding. At the basis of it all was the need to define our terms: what did we mean by 'religion'? The fundamental job of the *Everyman* series as laid down by those who gave it funds was to produce 'religious' documentaries. In the stranding system of the BBC, which divides human activities into recognizable categories such as 'Sport', 'Science', 'Arts', 'Natural History', the label seems easy to understand, so programme controllers tuning in to a programme from the religious department expected to see earnest men in clerical collars sitting in a circle and talking about spiritual matters, or the aforementioned ladies singing hymns, or people worshipping, or men in gowns swinging incense in a church setting. In other words, just as sports documentaries were about people engaging in sports or talking about them, religious documentaries had to be about people visibly engaging in, or discussing religious practices.

But we discovered, after making a few films of this kind, that we were missing out on something. A comedy programme which consisted of psychologists and sociologists discussing the nature and function of humour, or simply shots of audiences laughing, would fail as a comedy programme. Comedy programmes should make people laugh. And some of us began to feel that our job was not only to inform the audience about the nature of religious practices but also to convey and possibly even to excite the feeling of wonder, inspiration or merely recognition of otherness which is the first step in religious experience.

Most of the people working in the *Everyman* team during the years when I was its reporter were, like me, uncommitted agnostics – some in the original Huxleyan sense that they believed all claims to knowledge in the area of religion to be mistaken, since nothing can be known beyond material phenomena. Most, including myself, would have acknowledged the label in the more colloquial sense that we ourselves had not yet discovered a religious truth, without denying that others might. We were brought hard up against those others in every film we made, often in ways which challenged our assumptions about what it was we were investigating and how we should approach it.

A visit to South Dakota early in the series made me feel that the impartial, reasonable, concerned, investigative stance I was adopting might well be off-beam. We were looking at the religion of the Sioux Indians, and began by filming a traffic cop who started each day by hanging a packet of

Lucky Strike cigarettes from the branches of a tree. He did this, he told me, so that the Great Spirit would protect him from harm during the day. A burly, aggressive, full-blooded Sioux, with a gun at his hip, it was easy to believe him when he told me that his job put him at risk every day. In the traditions of his people, he said, an offering, usually of tobacco leaf, to Wakan Tanka, the Great Spirit, would be placed in a tree because the tree was the most noble and lasting of the living things in which the Great Spirit dwelt. As he roared off down the road on a powerful motorcycle, as seen in Hollywood films, blue light flashing for the camera, with a tiny red and white cigarette packet dancing in the breeze among twigs in the foreground, it made a colourful sequence to illustrate the survival of quaint primitive customs in the world's most powerful industrialized nation.

Better things were to come. I met a young, slim, half-Sioux pilot who had just returned from flying Phantom jets in Vietnam. He told me that, before setting out from the States, he had vowed to the Great Spirit that, if he returned safely, he would perform the sacred Sun Dance in gratitude. To perform the Sun Dance, a participant begins by piercing the pectoral muscles on each side of his chest with a sharp stick and passing thin leather thongs through the flesh. These are then tied to the top of a totem pole, and the dancer circles the pole, facing it and leaning back against the thongs until the leather tears through the flesh and he is freed. That an educated young man, highly trained in the technology needed to fly a supersonic aircraft in combat, should submit himself to primitive self-torture to comply with an ancient belief was another colourful illustration of the ongoing power of religion that was sure to satisfy the channel controller and help our audience figures. We could not film the Sun Dance, since the pilot had already performed it, but he opened his shirt for me on camera and showed his scars.

I felt we were doing a fine job at lending a sympathetic ear to exotic superstition when we set out for Bear Mountain to talk about the Vision Quest. Again the setting was superb.

The plain to the east of Rapid City was studded with concrete pads that house Minutemen missiles carrying the nuclear warheads which were the Pentagon's version of Lucky Strike in a tree. Bear Mountain rises in the middle of the plain and is a place sacred to the Sioux. Here their young men and women come in search of the vision. Red Cloud and Crazy Horse came here in their youth. So did Little Wolf and Sitting Bull. When I arrived with a television crew and a Sioux chief called Pete Catches Enemy, I was anticipating another session of sexy television with a noble savage recounting misty-eyed the long-lost dreams of his tribe as the B-52s from Ellsworth Air Force Base roared overhead.

But Pete did not look like a Sioux chief from central casting. True he had copper skin and a thin, beaked nose. But he was dressed in jeans, a plaid shirt and a well-scuffed ex-pilot's leather jacket. He wore on his head a fur trapper's cap with flaps over the ears. For half a day we climbed knee-deep in snow up the mountain to the summit, where there were a few pine trees and a pile of black rocks. Here, Pete told me, the young men – and sometimes women – of his tribe would come alone to seek a vision. They would dress only in a buffalo-hide cloak and would sit fasting under the open sky until the vision came. And why was the vision so important that they would go through solitude, hunger and freezing temperatures to find it? The answer put a dent in my complacency as a well-disposed Western liberal impartially investigating religious truth.

Until a person had a vision, Pete explained, that person is not mature, not really grown-up. The true nature of reality cannot be understood without personal experience of it. You can try to teach children that we are all somehow related to the world around us – that there is a spirit animating all things which we share – but they will hear your words without understanding you. Everyone must experience a vision to reach understanding.

And I realized how opposed our own educational system is to this. We teach the eradication of visions. Our learning consists of sharpening the rational cognitive faculties so that mysteries can be comprehended, cleared up. According to Piaget, that expert on the development of the cognitive faculties in children, education consists of liberating the developing mind of the child from an illusory view of reality. The most adult person in our society is the one who has given up fantasies, the one with the well-stocked mind and the analytical intelligence. Children, for us Westerners, are just inefficient adults.

Perhaps, just perhaps, it occurred to me after talking with Pete, religious realities were not accessible to impartial investigation, no matter how sympathetic. Perhaps a knowledge of religious practices did not bring one any closer to religious truth. Perhaps this truth cannot be understood second-hand. Perhaps this is what Jesus meant by telling people they must become as little children to enter the kingdom of heaven.

In Hollywood I went through an experience which I thought at the time was simply making a very interesting point about the relationship of mind and body; but it turned out to have a deeper relevance. We went to make a film about a tennis coach who had discovered a route to self-enlightenment through sport. Tim Galway had developed a new technique of teaching which involved, according to his best-selling book, *The Inner Game of Tennis*, listening to the body rather than the mind. This seemed to be a harmless piece of West Coast muddle-headed fantasy which might make an entertaining film on the fringes of supernatural, or at least super-physical, experience, so we took along a camera crew and booked me in for a series of lessons.

I was the ideal pupil, because I already knew a lot about the technique of playing tennis without having acquired any skills. When faced, in Fiji, by the social necessity to take part in a sport I always thought slightly effeminate, I had reacted in the usual way and given myself a stiff course of reading about it. There are plenty of books on the technique of playing tennis. I had studied the diagrams showing the grip on the racquet 'like a hammer', and knew how far apart my feet should be, how high to toss the ball for the service and when to hit it. I had lots of knowledge but no ability. I was physically strong and capable of hitting the ball hard, but without any control over where it went.

So when Tim Galway wheeled a supermarket trolley of bright yellow balls on to a sunbaked tennis court in Hollywood one morning in the early summer of 1975 and began lobbing them at me, telling me to hit them back over the net, I managed to lose quite a few. Some hit the net, some went vertically into the air; one shattered the cameraman's glasses with a direct hit; none, I think, landed in the square where they were supposed to go.

Then he told me to stop trying to return the balls – simply to watch them. He kept on lobbing them over and asking me questions: 'Which side of the ball is the shadow on?' 'Does the ball spin faster *before* or *after* it hits the ground?' 'What colour is the shadow?' I had to concentrate hard on looking at the balls as they came towards me and had no time to watch what happened when I hit them. After about five minutes of this, he stopped and pointed out that, of the last twenty balls he had thrown at me, eighteen had come back about two inches over the net and landed exactly where they were supposed to.

Then came the sermon. So long as my mind was engaged in trying to hit the balls back in the right way, I couldn't do it. When my mind was distracted by all the questions, so that I looked hard at the balls without trying to hit them back, my body took over and I succeeded. So the lesson was: listen to your body, not your mind. I was impressed, but not convinced.

Then we moved on to the service. This I could never quite manage, because I couldn't see, over the net, the square in which the ball is supposed to land. He put a chair on the spot I should aim for and told me to try to hit the chair. Then came the interesting bit. I had to shout to him how far short or long or to the left or right a ball had fallen *without trying to correct it*. The first shot was a couple of yards to the left, and I shouted this before having another go. This time it landed a couple of yards to the right. 'You're trying to correct,' Tim shouted. 'Stop it. Just tell me how far out you were.' And we went on. At first I found it impossible not to correct; but when I tried to correct I overcorrected. When I managed simply to register how I'd gone wrong and did nothing consciously to correct it I got it right. After a couple of hours on the court I had to accept that we had demonstrated the truth of a proposition I should have thought ludicrous: the body can sometimes act more efficiently to achieve an aim when it is not under the control of the conscious mind.

Back in England, on 1 December 1976 I did something so completely irrational that my conscious mind must have been disconnected. I remarried. My first marriage had failed, and I had long looked forward to spending the rest of my life in seclusion with my books and records, emerging only to make whatever money I needed to live simply and alone. But I had come to realize an inconvenient fact: I felt fully alive only when I was with Felicia. We lived together for a time and were happy. There seemed no reason to change our relationship, and many reasons against second marriage: it was recognized as the triumph of hope over experience; statistics were against its survival; nothing could be more irrational than to make again a promise which you have proved yourself unable to keep. So, there being no earthly reason why we should, we decided to marry. It was not only completely irrational, it was the best decision I ever made.

About this time I interviewed a Jesuit priest who had a doctorate in mystical theology from Sophia University, in Tokyo, had written several books on Christian and Zen mysticism, and was an expert on meditation. He was William Johnston, and we talked about his latest book, *Silent Music:*

The Science of Meditation. At the time, transcendental meditation, introduced to the West by Maharishi Mahesh Yogi and given a publicity boost by the Beatles, was the trendy way to self-realization. It was popular not because it promised spiritual enlightenment but because it was advertised as a way to develop human potential. This meant that people who practised it would do more efficiently whatever they chose to do. Business tycoons were slipping off their handmade shoes and sitting in cross-legged silence from Wall Street to Tokyo in the hope of boosting profits. Overstretched currency dealers were seeking to calm their minds by emptying them. Enervated pop stars were tapping into new sources of energy by squatting in darkened rooms.

The aspect of this new vogue for an ancient practice which most interested me was its claim to be more scientific than mystical. A new jargon had sprung up, and people talked of 'ASC' for 'altered states of consciousness'; 'MSC' for 'meditation states of consciousness', 'HSC' for 'higher states of consciousness' and 'EIA' for 'enhanced internal awareness'. The new science was slotted into evolutionary doctrines through what was called the 'filter theory'. This proposed that the brain and nervous systems are fitted with restrictive filters which prevent total reality from entering: only such information as is necessary for biological survival reaches us. If it were not for these protective barriers we should be swamped by information of no survival value and our existence would be threatened. Humankind cannot bear very much reality.

These protective barriers can be removed by drugs or certain illnesses. Some people – the psychics – are born with deficient barriers and are open to telepathy, clairvoyance and other parapsychological sources of information. The natural and gradual way of opening the filters is through meditation, which welcomes the inflow of reality and expands the mind. The process was shown to be experimentally repeatable and linked to minute electrical impulses given off by the brain and recordable on an electroencephalograph. Four kinds of brain waves were identified. Beta waves are the most common in waking hours, when the active mind is reacting to outside stimuli; these measure thirteen or more cycles per second. Alpha waves, which measure eight to twelve cycles per second, are an indication of relaxed awareness. Theta waves, of four to seven cycles per second, indicate drowsiness; and delta waves, from zero to four cycles per second, are given off in deep sleep.

These classifications, apart from indicating that the scientist who made them had only a vague knowledge of the Greek alphabet, are significant in that they indicate an objective, empirical and recordable relationship between altered states of consciousness. It was no surprise to anybody to be told that people are sometimes awake, sometimes drowsy and sometimes asleep. The change in electrical activity of the brain in these three different conditions is predictable and not particularly interesting. But the claims relating to alpha waves were novel and fascinating.

About 10 per cent of the population of the United States, it was claimed, are non-alpha producers. The best alpha producers are people who practise meditation, the champions in this field being the Zen masters, followed by the Yogi and Christian monks. The altered states of consciousness which alpha waves indicate are the ones which are mind-expanding. These are the states susceptible to the inflow of religious experience. I was professionally committed to searching out and evaluating religious experience. It seemed worth trying a few experiments.

The quickest way into alpha production is by injecting direct into the bloodstream a mind-altering drug such as LSD. Apart from the difficulty in getting hold of LSD, this seemed to me to have a fatal objection: if a new state of consciousness is produced by a drug, how can we tell whether this is an expansion or a distortion? The little green men which a friend of mine in Fiji used to see at the foot of his bed after downing a bottle of Scotch were visible to him only when the alcohol was in his bloodstream. We concluded from this not that they were actually there all the time and detectable by the organs of perception only when their sensitivity was enhanced by the whisky, but simply that when drunk he saw things which did not exist. So I tried simple meditation.

Having read several books on the subject, I sat cross-legged (not difficult after fifteen years in Fiji) in a darkened room and gazed at the flame of a candle. The next step, according to my instructions, was to empty my mind. This I found impossible. As I looked at the flame, an image came immediately to me of a diagram from my school chemistry textbook. It showed a candle flame with a thin glass tube with one end in the dark area near the wick and the other beyond the edge of the flame. If a lit match is applied to the upper end of the tube, the gas being ducted upwards will ignite, producing a tiny flame at the end of the tube. This proves something, though I had forgotten what. Having banished the image, I then noticed what a very restless object a candle flame is. At the peak it trembles and wavers constantly, the tip divides and changes shape; at the base, however hard you look, you can't detect where the flame actually begins. A candle flame is a fascinating and stimulating object, part of it straddling the worlds of existence and non-existence. I gazed at mine for ten minutes or so and felt alive and interested in the world about me. There was no hint of enhanced internal awareness, or EIA, and my alpha-wave reading must have been at zero.

So I tried an orange, as recommended by some of my books on the ancient practices of yoga. I should have been able to lose myself in contemplating its roundness, its restful colour and its evenly dimpled skin. But my orange had subtle variations of colour, from pale yellow through touches of olive green to a deeply satisfying but slightly mottled ochre. And it had a small oval paper sticker announcing that it came from Israel, so in no time at all I was pondering the morality of the Balfour Declaration and the ownership of the Golan Heights.

My experiments with meditation proved that I found it difficult to enter a state of relaxed concentration using the approved channels. Either I had been born with preternaturally robust filters or my EIA faculties were atrophied, or both. Candle flames and oranges had brought me no nearer to God, so somebody decided I should have a go at fasting.

Going without food as a stimulus to spiritual progress is well established in all the great religious traditions. Hindu sannyasi go through long periods without eating anything, and often look as if they do; in Islam, the period of Ramadan is spent without eating or drinking anything between sunrise and the appearance of the first stars at nightfall; the Jews are rigorous fasters. Christians seemed uncertain.

The fasts of Christ as recorded in the New Testament are well known, and the Roman Catholic Church has incorporated fasting into its regular observances. The *Catholic Encyclopaedia* finds that here the Church is in accord with the laws of nature:

> Moralists are one in maintaining that a natural law inculcates the necessity of fasting because every rational creature is bound to labour intelligently for the subjugation of concupiscence ... Amongst the means naturally subserving this purpose, fasting lays claim to a place of primary importance.

And the Roman Catholics are characteristically precise in defining what constitutes fasting: my tomes on moral theology tell me that two ounces of meat or four ounces of soup constitute a 'grave violation' of a fast.

The Church of England seems characteristically uncertain. Although an Elizabethan statute forbade the eating of meat on Wednesdays, Fridays and Saturdays, it provided not only penalties for non-compliance but also rules for the issuing of licences to avoid the prohibition. The Book of Common Prayer contains a table of 'Vigils, Fasts, and Days of Abstinence' but no specific directions as to their observance.

And, although fasting was taken up with enthusiasm by the Oxford Movement, Protestant theologians tended to reject it as redolent of 'smells and bells'. Their attitude is well put by an unsigned article, clearly written by a well-bred Englishman, in the eleventh edition of the *Encyclopaedia Britannica*:

> Habitual temperance will generally be found to be much more beneficial than occasional fasting. It is extremely questionable, in particular, whether fasting be so efficient as it is sometimes supposed to be in protecting against temptation to fleshly sin. The practice has a well-ascertained tendency to excite the imagination; and insofar as it disturbs that healthy and well-balanced interaction of body and mind which is the best, or at least the normal, condition for the practice of virtue, it is to be deprecated rather than encouraged.

When we took the decision that I, together with half a dozen volunteers, should undergo a fast as the subject of a religious documentary, we were therefore uncertain as to its likely effects: the Roman Catholics held that it would subjugate our concupiscence, but the Protestants that it might excite our imaginations and threaten our virtue.

More televisually promising were the notions of social anthropologists that primitive man underwent fasts to bring on at will certain abnormal nervous conditions favourable to the seeing of those visions and the dreaming of those dreams which are supposed to give the soul direct access to the objective realities of the spirit world. We had heard of such practices among the Sioux in South Dakota seeking their spirit visions on the peak of Bear Mountain, and Aldous Huxley had explained in *Heaven and Hell* how they operate in biological terms:

> The first result of an inadequate diet is a lowering of the efficiency of the brain as an instrument for biological survival. The undernourished person tends to be affected by anxiety, depression, hypochondria and feelings of anxiety. He

is also liable to see visions; for when the cerebral reducing valve has its efficiency reduced much (biologically speaking) useless material flows into consciousness from 'out there' in Mind-at-Large.

So it was with high expectations that I set out one Monday morning in the summer of 1979 for a remote farm in the southern countryside. A medical team would supervise the fast, which would last until Saturday. I had, of course, read all the available books on the experience we were about to go through. I knew that, in fasting, the liver would break down fatty acids into ketone bodies and that these were then used, in the absence of glucose, to supply energy to the brain. This was a process known as ketosis. It produced a characteristic and unmistakable sweet smell on the breath, and the *Penguin Medical Encyclopaedia* even suggested that the odour of ketosis on the breath after prolonged fasting may well have been the 'odour of sanctity' reported as issuing from the saints. A researcher had pointed out that one of the ketone bodies, called beta-hydroxybutiric acid, is normally negligible in the adult brain but an active force in the brain of a child. He went on to suggest that this could be the chemical base of the sense of wonder which adults lose. Was I about to recover it?

We lived in small rooms each containing a single bed, a table and a chair. We were allowed as much bottled water as we wanted – sparkling or still – but no food of any kind, and the doctor in charge, who was researching the effects of ketosis on the body, took daily blood samples to check that nobody cheated. We were weighed on arrival.

Each day the camera crew and producer would come to the farm with a different stimulus to our spiritual sensitivities. A monk told us of his experiences with fasting, admitting that, though his fasts lasted longer than ours, they were not total. A tantric yoga teacher put us through a series of yogic postures designed to awaken spiritual energies. One afternoon we spent listening to Mahler symphonies, lying on mats in a darkened room. I had recently completed a film about jogging and, being bitten by the habit, went off for a daily run before and after work.

My books had told me that for the first three days I should feel pangs of hunger. I did, especially on going to bed at night. Then the decision had to be taken whether to assuage them by drinking bottles of water, which meant getting up at intervals all night, or to try for uninterrupted sleep, which was hard to achieve with a nagging ache in the stomach area. I had a cassette recorder by my bed with earphones, and usually managed to fall asleep to the sound of music. The books went on to say that, after three days, the hunger would subside and I should feel at peace. It did not, and I still felt hungry. Fortunately, part of my job was to interview the other participants, so I was constantly distracted from my own discomfort by talking about theirs.

We reacted very differently. One man, in his mid-thirties with an interest in fringe religions, woke screaming one night and said he had dreamed that his room was slowly filling with water; a middle-aged woman thought she was having a heart attack. Nobody was pitched into religious enthusiasm by the various stimuli supplied. We all felt light-headed, slightly more serious about life than usual, and tended, I think, to take things slowly and deliberately – like people who are slightly drunk.

The crew would arrive each day about eight o'clock. At about eleven they would begin to nudge each other and explain rather lamely that they had to go elsewhere for about half an hour. This was the coffee break, and it was followed by the lunch break, which was taken in the same surreptitious manner. The producer had forbidden them to mention either food or drink in any context. We took this lightly enough and were not particularly worried about the idea of food, though out of sheer bravado I did make the mistake of spending the afternoon of Wednesday swapping recipes with a young woman volunteer. This must have caused some sort of excessive eruption of the gastric juices, because we both felt quite ill for a time.

On that third day we were asked what we should like to eat at the end of the fast. A banquet was planned at which we were allowed to choose any dish, and we were to be filmed eating it. I plumped for (bravado again) a twelve-ounce T-bone steak with four fried eggs and a pint of stout. By Thursday evening I felt less sure about this, and by the end of Friday I decided it was a bad idea. I ended up asking for a strange concoction which, without discussion, we had all come to lust after: chopped vegetables boiled for at least two hours and served in their water. When, on Saturday morning with a camera inches from my face, I raised the first spoonful to my lips, I wept.

On the last day, in a final attempt to push myself into some sort of unusual experience, I had run at a fair pace for eight miles round the country lanes. I remember feeling physically light and slightly mentally slow, but otherwise normal. The run took about an hour, which was my normal time for the distance. I felt tired, but saw no visions. It seemed that, as an experiment in mind expansion, fasting had failed me or I had failed fasting. I had lost thirteen pounds in weight and gained not an ounce of spiritual awareness. I was driven home in a taxi, protesting that I was perfectly capable of driving myself. My wife tells me that for the following two weeks I wandered round the house as if I were sleepwalking and refused to eat anything but boiled vegetables.

It seemed to me that an incapacity of some kind lay at the heart of my inability to accept the realities which religious people urged on me and apparently were able to rejoice in and find of supreme value. I felt sure that I was not opposed to the claims of spirituality. I accepted that religion was an ancient and powerful force to which men and women had responded for as long as humanity had existed. I knew enough theology to realize that grace was a free gift from God, and that grace was necessary to faith. I had read of the hunger in the heart that drove people to God, the unsatisfied longing that could find rest only in him. But I had to admit that I had no such hunger and no longing, merely a quite serious intellectual curiosity about the whole business. So long as faith depended on a need, I was likely to miss out. Of course, theologians told me that God provided the need in the first place, so I could only conclude that he had not yet got around to it in my case.

But we received one day in the *Everyman* office a leaflet advertising a meditation ashram in Chobham, Surrey, which made an unusual claim. The guru to whom the ashram was devoted had the power to transmit instant enlightenment, irrespective, it seemed, of the state of mind of the recipient. He was, the leaflet claimed, 'a Perfect Being and a direct channel for the dispensation of Divine Grace. He is a True Guru possessing the power to awaken a seeker's Kundalini by touch, word, look or thought. This transmission of Divine Shakti (conscious energy) from the Guru to the disciple is known as Shaktipat Diksha.'

I remembered hearing about Kundalini during my yogic period in Fiji. She is the female energy in the form of a snake that lies coiled at the base of the spine. She can be awakened, I had been taught, only by a long course of *pranayama*, or breathing exercises coupled with yogic postures, which I had followed for some months with considerable physical but no perceptible spiritual benefits. The guru who would be visiting Chobham seemed to be able to awaken Kundalini on the instant and with no effort on the disciple's part. And the benefits were considerable. The leaflet went on:

As a result of the awakening of his Kundalini the seeker experiences effortless meditation and extraordinary changes within which affect him physically, emotionally, intellectually and spiritually. In his meditation he commences to enjoy infinite marvels and secrets, most mysterious knowledge, love as deep as the ocean and an inner strength as solid as a mountain. In his inner life he will notice release of nervous tension, less worry and anxiety, better health, sharper intellect, greater self-confidence and a beautiful expansion of love from the personal to the Universal.

The most important aspect of the guru's powers for me was that he could apparently awaken my Kundalini without my help. As I seemed to be resistant to all stimuli to enlightenment, this sounded promising. We arranged to visit the ashram during the period when he would be in residence, so that I could interview him and ask for instant enlightenment.

Swami Muktananda Paramahansa was a wonderful advertisement for his teaching: a short, bright-eyed man wearing a red knitted cap and red socks, he talked in a quiet, almost shy manner, with none of the assertive, foot-in-the-door urgency that I had come to associate with missionaries. Although he had at the time sixty-two meditation centres in North America and flew between them and his main ashram in India in a chartered 747, he was not an overbearing personality. But he was impressive: warm, emotional, enthusiastic and far more interested in everybody else than in the impression he made on them.

We talked about religion, particularly Hinduism and yogic practices and the ways in which they could be relevant to life today. Then we came to the question of Shaktipat. 'Can you really', I asked him, 'enlighten people by a touch?' He nodded, smiling. 'And will you', I went on, 'enlighten me – on Thursday?' (We had arranged a camera crew for the day.) He leaned forward and looked me in the eye, not piercingly, not even solemnly, but with a light smile: 'By Friday morning', he said, 'you will have no more questions.'

On Thursday morning our little crew – cameraman, assistant cameraman, sound man, sparks, producer, producer's assistant and I – arrived at the ashram to find an immense marquee filled with about 400 people sitting on mats in lines across the floor, cross-legged and silent. A place had been reserved for me at the front, and I quietly sat there, not without a touch of complacency at being able to demonstrate to the guru's followers that I could manage a half-lotus position without a struggle. At about half past ten the guru entered at the far end of the tent – accompanied, I was a touch alarmed to see, by his own camera crew. They were from America, and their equipment was more compact, modern and expensive than ours.

He began giving Shaktipat to the lines of sitting followers, and I watched with increasing tension. Some he touched lightly as he passed. Others he seemed to hold by the tops of their heads and to move them gently backwards and forwards as he chanted until a spasm shook them and they fell back with a cry and lay wriggling and twitching. By the time he was getting close to where I was sitting there were dozens of people shivering in ecstasy on the ground, some coiled like snakes, some stiff and straight, some quietly weeping, some chanting mantras. There was increasing noise, movement, excitement, and I looked at the ground in front of me and concentrated on emptying my mind. I knew that the cameras – his and ours – would record everything that happened when he came to me, and I was trying hard not to let this thought inhibit me from responding spontaneously to him.

He squatted in front of me. He rubbed a little scented oil on the space between my eyes. He closed my right nostril with his thumb and blew gently into the left. His breath was lightly scented. Then he closed the left nostril and blew into the right. Then he took a large fan of peacock's feathers and struck me lightly on the head three times. Then he held my head and moved it gently backwards and forwards. And what did I feel? I felt as if somebody had rubbed oil on my forehead, blown up my nostrils, and struck me on the head with a peacock feather fan. Nothing more.

By some spiritual ricochet, the force directed at me struck my producer. He was converted on the spot, became a devotee of the guru, and left the BBC. I remained adamantly unenchanted.

But there was another opportunity to succumb to the spell of the East. An even more famous and successful celebrity guru had a workshop in London: Bhagwan Shree Rajneesh – he of the 180 Rolls-Royces. His message was that mankind has been forced into neurosis by centuries of sexual oppression; that the way to freedom is through indulgence. No wonder he had 180 Rolls-Royces. They enrolled me for a course.

It is easy to satirize Rajneesh, and this has been done very well many times. His teachings were not so much a faith as a technique. In the practice of that technique the 'me' generation found a freedom to be self-indulgent under the approving eyes of their spiritual mentors. After generations of furtive couplings known only to the recording angel, they were encouraged to bang away with the full approval of 'holy' men and women who had themselves been released from the bonds of a 'false' religion. Not surprisingly, the teachings were used to justify abandoned self-indulgence and gained international acclaim. At their heart there is something of value. But first to the practice.

We went one morning to the upper floor of an office block in central London. A large room had been carpeted wall to wall with a thick grey soft covering, the purpose of which was to become evident. As usual, I was to be put through the experience and recorded by the camera. First we (there were about twenty other men and women) were invited to take off all our clothes and put on white ankle-length garments rather like Victorian nightdresses. Then we stood about in the large room listening to gentle Eastern music and breathing slowly and deeply. We were offered blindfolds, so that we would not be distracted by what others were doing but concentrate on ourselves. The message was all about concentrating on ourselves. After about ten minutes the pulse of the music quickened and we were told to jump up and down in time with it and to breathe in short, shallow panting to quicken the pulse. The music reached a climax of frenzy, and we had to fling ourselves on the ground (hence the thick-pile carpet)

and release our tensions by shouting all the words we had
wanted to say all our lives but had kept bottled up inside us.

I noticed (I had rejected the blindfold) a middle-aged
Anglican priest, whose dog collar I had spotted before he
climbed into his nightshirt, rolling on the carpet and shouting
'Fuck! Fuck! Fuck!' As I looked around at the others, 'Fuck!'
seemed to be the favoured word, though a sedate lady from
the home counties lay on her back at my side and muttered in
a cut-glass accent, 'Bugger.' Not to be left out, I flung myself
on the ground, but I was completely unable to think of
anything I had been bottling up. Either my repressions were
too deep-seated to be dislodged by hyperventilation or I had
a vocally uninhibited past. I rolled about a bit and then sat up
to watch the others.

Most of them were managing quite well with the taboo
expletives, though they didn't enlarge my vocabulary and I
was surprised at the impoverished range of the words they
had been longing to utter. After about three minutes things
quietened down and soothing sitar music came through the
loudspeakers, followed by a recorded sermon from Bhagwan
himself. He spoke in a gentle, intimate tone of voice, and
what he had to say seemed to me to contain religious insight:

> You will need a change; rather a mutation. Unless *you* are
> different, tantra cannot be understood, because tantra is not
> an intellectual proposition: it is an experience.
>
> To tackle a problem intellectually is very easy. But to tackle
> a problem existentially, not just to think about it but to live it
> through . . . is difficult. That is, to know love, one will have
> to be in love. That is dangerous, because you will not remain
> the same. The experience will change you.
>
> Yoga is suppression with awareness; tantra is indulgence
> with awareness.

That final message, I discovered as we changed out of our
nightdresses, was what prompted one young devotee to
attend nightly sessions. He told me, 'It doesn't half help pull
the birds!'

The published works of Bhagwan Shree Rajneesh are mainly the transcripts of his impromptu lectures. They tend to ramble, as reflects the easy style of his delivery, but they are rich in provoking ideas. He quotes not only, as you might expect, Annie Besant, Khalil Gibran, Meher Baba and Krishnamurti but also Sartre, Nietzsche, Hume, Dostoevsky and Bertrand Russell. At the heart of all his teaching is the constant insistence that religion can never be understood with the mind but only through direct experience.

So we are back to what I had come to think of as the Wesley's Warm Glow Syndrome. As every Methodist knows, John Wesley had recorded that on 24 May 1738 at quarter to nine in the evening he felt his heart 'strangely warmed' and knew at once that Christ had taken away his sins. I quite frequently met people who had a similar experience to report. It seemed clear to me that such religious experiences were wholly authoritative for the subjects and totally without authority for anyone else. The effects of these experiences sometimes endured. We had often dealt with people during the *Everyman* series who were changed by some personal revelation that had a total and a lasting conviction for them. In making films about revivalist meetings with Billy Graham and Louis Palau I had talked to many who had 'given their lives to Jesus' on an impulse which seemed generated by the atmosphere of the meeting; often the change had proved lasting. Whatever had happened was certainly real for them.

I once talked to an ex-prisoner from Dartmoor jail who told me that he had decided one day to murder one of the guards. He stole a strip of metal – I think it was the hinge of a door – from the workshop, and for weeks, he gradually sharpened it until it had a razor edge. He kept it hidden under his mattress. Finally he picked the day when the guard would be on duty and went to bed relishing the thought of slitting his throat the next morning. He was, he told me, awakened from sleep by the presence of three men at the foot of the bed. One of them pointed at the man in the middle and said, 'Fred, this is Jesus.' Fred was half asleep. 'I didn't believe 'im,' he told me, 'because Jesus was dressed just like you and me. I mean, 'e didn't 'ave a rope rahnd 'is 'ead like the Arabs, like you sees in the pictures.' But when Jesus spoke to Fred he was convinced. Next day he threw away his knife and behaved like an exemplary prisoner to the end of his sentence. Since his release from jail he had devoted himself to preaching the Word. Fred's story was colourful and made good television. He spoke with evident sincerity, and I thought that at least he had taken the trouble to convince himself before trying to convince the rest of us. As an argument for the truth of revelation, Fred's story left the hearer with an open mind.

But there was an approach to religious experience which had the colouring of scientific impartiality. And, because I had not quite discarded the schoolboy conviction that the sciences describe the world as it is, whereas the arts deal only with what we wish it were or hope it might be, I was excited by it. In the Gifford Lectures of 1965, Sir Alister Hardy, an Oxford biologist, had attempted the first steps in a natural history of religious experience. He had founded the Religious Experience Research Unit at Manchester College, Oxford, to collect material relating to religious experience on which he hoped to base a scientific study of what he held to be a universal human phenomenon.

I met Sir Alister at his house in north Oxford in May 1978 to plan a television documentary about the work of the Unit. I had been warned by a few hard-nosed determinist biologists at the BBC Natural History Unit to expect an old man in the terminal stages of mental decline. He had, after all scandalized many of his colleagues by proposing that there was a divine element in the natural processes of the world and that serious scientists should spend time and money studying it. I met a bright, courteous, slightly eccentric man who arrived riding what appeared to be a butcher's bicycle but who showed no sign that his intellect might have lost its edge.

He reminded me that religious experience was a near-universal phenomenon in human society, and referred me to Aldous Huxley's claim for the Perennial Philosophy:

> The phrase was coined by Leibniz; but the thing – the metaphysic that recognizes a divine Reality substantial to the world of things and lives and minds; the psychology that finds in the soul something similar to, or even identical with, divine Reality; the ethic that places man's final end in the knowledge of the immanent and transcendental Ground of all being – the thing is immemorial and universal.

He went on to say that, since religious experience was common, and profoundly influenced human behaviour, it was a proper object of scientific study – though scientists could make no valid judgement on whether or not such experience reflected a transcendental reality. As a biologist, he thought it quite possible that the rapture of spiritual experience might be a valid part of natural history. What was needed – and the Religious Experience Research Unit was set up to meet this need – was an accumulation of data on which scientific theory could be based. He compared the work of the Unit to that of the field workers in the early stages of the natural sciences who collected observational material on the appearance and behaviour of plants and animals on which later biologists erected their structures of theory.

The Unit had been set up in the belief that there is overwhelming evidence, which can be collected and submitted to the scientifically thinking world, that (1) religious experience has played and can play an important part in human behaviour, (2) there is a consistent pattern in the records of such experience and (3) on many occasions men and women have, by what they call divine help or grace, achieved what they and others who knew them would have regarded as beyond their normal capabilities. Questionnaires were distributed to people who believed that they had had 'extra-sensory contact with a Power which is greater than and in part lies beyond the individual self'.

To me, the most interesting, and surprising, aspect of their findings is that people seem to have religious experiences not, as psychological theory might suggest, at times of great stress, anxiety or need. Most of the reported experiences were from comfortable middle-class people, and they occurred at times of ease approaching tranquillity. They could not be comforting illusions projected from the unconscious mind to appease uncontrollable urges or irrepressible anxieties. Religious experience was discovered to be surprisingly widespread, to the point where it was inappropriate to think of it as abnormal, and, most strangely to me, it was associated not with neurotic inadequates but with healthy, confident people, whose lives were permanently enhanced by it.

As I was not one of them, I had to look elsewhere for religious truth.

Chapter Six

Roman Catholicism had been the only branch of Christianity in which I felt a rational adult could take a serious interest, and it kept its attraction for me until the last of a series of films I made on Catholic subjects. Much of this attraction had to do with an insistence on the rational basis of faith and the rejection of religious experience. Ronald Knox, a brilliant scholar whose intelligence carried him into the Catholic Church, wrote, 'all this modern talk about religious experience is cant; that is to say when it is used for apologetic purposes'. Knox rebelled against the assertion that a personal religious experience had any objective authority. He says somewhere that he had never had such an experience, and would not trust it if he did. I admired his candour.

In no proceeding is the scrupulous and meticulous scholarship and rational scepticism of the Catholic Church better demonstrated than in the process for canonization. I was able to follow this procedure closely in a documentary we made about the canonization of John Ogilvie, a seventeenth-century martyr.

Ogilvie had been executed at Glasgow in 1615, and the cause for his beatification – the first stage in canonization – was opened in Rome in 1628. Such is the leisurely pace of events in the Eternal City that the process took 300 years to complete, and he was not pronounced the Blessed John Ogilvie until 22 December 1929. The next step is canonization, which is not turning a man into a saint but recognizing officially that he was (and is) one. In furtherance of this, a process was reassumed in 1965. What was then required was evidence that the Blessed John Ogilvie had worked a miracle.

A Glasgow man, John Fagan, had fallen ill in 1965 and was discovered to have a huge cancerous growth in his stomach, so large that it could not be completely removed. He had been sent home to die, and in the early months of 1967 he was visited twice a day by his doctor and given injections of morphine. His home was in the parish of the Blessed John Ogilvie, and his priest, aware of the process for canonization and its requirements, told his wife to pin a medal of Ogilvie on his pyjamas and led the church congregation in specific prayers to the Blessed Martyr that John Fagan might recover.

On the evening of 4 March the doctor called and said that Fagan could not last the night. He would return next day to sign the death certificate. Fagan's wife sat by his bedside all night, and the next morning could find no sign of life: no pulse, breathing or heartbeat. She went into the kitchen and then heard her husband calling her. 'I'm hungry,' he said. She made him a boiled egg. He recovered completely.

All these details were given in evidence sent to the postulator of the cause for canonization in Rome, a scholarly Jesuit, who then arranged for an investigation of the most awesome scrupulousness to eradicate any possibility that the recovery of John Fagan might have been due to natural causes. A panel of three doctors in Scotland scrutinized all the medical reports from Fagan's family doctor and the hospital. They then sent these, with their observations, to Rome, where they were examined by doctors who specialized in cancer. Then Fagan was examined by two different panels of doctors, again specialists in cancer, who sent their reports to the postulator. Finally, a medical commission set up by the Sacred Congregation for the Causes of Saints, consisting of nine doctors from different nations, examined the whole of the evidence and prepared nine individual reports for the Sacred Congregation. A member of that Congregation was the 'devil's advocate', whose duty it was to root out errors, challenge assertions which were based on insufficient evidence, and put counter-arguments.

After an investigation which had lasted for nine years the Congregation ruled that Fagan's recovery could not possibly be attributed to natural causes. Then the Congressus Particularis, a theological board consisting of five academic theologians and four members of the Congregation for the Causes of Saints, sat to confirm that (1) the non-natural event was a miracle and (2) it was caused by the intervention of the Blessed John Ogilvie. They had to be satisfied, for example, that no other saint had been prayed to for the recovery of John Fagan. They eventually pronounced themselves satisfied, and the ceremony of canonization was held in St Peter's on 17 October 1976.

I was there with a camera crew to record the celebrations. The parish priest, Father Reilly, I remember, had arranged for a special consignment of Ogilvie tartan to be shipped out; there were Ogilvie medals with the date of canonization stamped on the face, and Father Reilly brought with him the bottle of 1811 Napoleon Brandy which he had been saving to open on the day when John Ogilvie was proclaimed a saint. The high drama of the ceremony in St Peter's when the Pope finally proclaimed the name of the newly recognized saint in the presence of the man he had saved from death was exhilarating. It was the culmination of a process which had taken three and a half centuries. A shining faith was evident in the faces of the parishioners from Glasgow. I thought of the comment Shaw puts into the mouth of his archbishop in St Joan: 'A miracle . . . is an event which creates faith. That is the purpose and nature of miracles.'

My next dealings with the Catholics were in the situation which showed them to the best advantage: I went to Poland. We were there to make a film about an ideological struggle. After a generation of Communist rule, the Poles were the most Catholic people in Europe, giving the lie to the old adage about *cuius regio eius religio*. Over 90 per cent of them were practising Catholics, and the highly efficient and tireless atheist propaganda from the State had made no impression on their faith. I interviewed Party officials in Warsaw. No, they said, they did not any longer teach that religion was a device of the capitalist system to anaesthetize the workers against the injustices they were suffering. They had come to terms with the fact that religion was an inexplicable but enduring private peculiarity for which a government had to make provision. Since the Churches had evolved to cater for this human need, let them get on with it, so long as they did not try to interfere in the running of the country.

At the parish level I heard a different story. A French-speaking priest told me that his people were struggling constantly against the hostile propaganda of the government, which controlled the press, radio and television. Priests were allowed to preach only inside their churches and, since some older churches were falling into decay, the area for religious activities was gradually being eroded. Planning permission for new churches was always refused. In the countryside the farmers had evolved a technique for coping with the problem. A farmer would apply for planning permission for a large garage to house his tractor. It would be built by the community and completed at night, when, unseen by the police, a cross would be fixed to the gable end and the parish priest would bless the building as a church. Since the authorities would not pull down a consecrated building, the area for permitted religious activities had been enlarged.

The priest was a shining optimist about the position of the Church in Poland. It was thriving, he said, because the people could see it as the country's one champion of justice against the oppressions of the communists. And he quoted Voltaire at me: 'An enemy of the Church all his life,' he said, 'Voltaire spoke the truest words about her that have ever been heard. He said, "If you want to destroy the Church, give her power and give her money." '

I remember going to bed that night, Monday 16 October 1978, and thinking about those words. About how the Christian Church has, down the centuries, survived persecution magnificently but seems unable to survive prosperity. How the blood of the martyrs has been the seed of the Church but the great destructive upheaval of the Reformation was mainly an attack on its riches and possessions. I was drifting off to sleep, having brought these sweeping thoughts down to a petty personal level, reflecting that since you apparently have to be poor and needy to swallow Christianity I was unlikely to make it even on BBC rates of pay, when my door burst open and the producer rushed in followed by a breathless cameraman with news that was eventually to end the long allure which the Catholic Church had held for me: the BBC World Service had announced from Rome that the first ever Polish Pope had been elected. Karol Wojtyla was the latest successor to St Peter.

We roused the rest of the crew and the interpreter, and in a couple of elderly vans on loan from Polish Television we drove through the night from Warsaw to Cracow, the city of Cardinal Wojtyla. We wanted to record the reactions when the city awoke to the news of his election. The dawn had broken as we pulled up in the street outside his office. Somebody had put a chair in the window on the first floor and on it a large photograph of Karol Wojtyla in cardinal's robes. A crowd of men were smoking and talking sombrely in the street and occasionally looking up at it. When we climbed up to his office there were a few priests standing about in small groups in the room and whispering to each other. It was as if somebody had died. I looked on his desk and saw the diary opened for that week. Among the pencilled entries was one for the following morning for a filmed interview with the BBC. He would not be able to keep that, or any other of his appointments. He would never be able to return again to that desk, to that office, to his former life. It was indeed as if somebody had died. One of his closest friends said to me that morning, 'They have taken our best man. Simply that. Our best.'

The same friend seems to have been responsible for news of our film filtering through to the Vatican, and we were invited there to show it privately to the Pope. I was conscious of coming into contact with a healthy, intelligent, enthusiastic but humble, holy and good man who reawakened my interest in Catholicism. He seemed to be confidently in possession of a truth, and I was curious to learn what it was. I read the various biographies of him as they appeared, and his own books as they were republished. This was surely a mature, intelligent man without need of a psychological prop. And yet he had a secure, inspiring faith and was well able to express and defend it.

Karol Wojtyla, as everyone soon learned, was a scholar, a university professor who wrote poetry; an athlete who loved to ski and swam every morning; a freedom fighter who led his students against the oppressions of a totalitarian power. When he took office as Pope, there was a rush of blood to the head of the world's press: the head of the largest religious denomination on earth was portrayed as a combination of Charlton Heston and Isaiah Berlin with a dash of Gandhi thrown in: A Man for our Times! A twentieth-century Pope!

The press soon came to realize that they had misjudged the man. In the months that followed his election things started to go wrong for them: the freedom fighter from Poland went to Latin America and told his priests there to stay out of the struggle for human rights; the university professor, committed to the free inquiring spirit of the intellect, silenced Hans Küng, the most internationally famous of Catholic teachers, for expressing unorthodox opinions. The Man for our Times launched a campaign against practices which had become accepted as the norms of our day: birth control, abortion and divorce. He forced his priests and nuns, who were beginning to adopt the more relaxed styles of our day, back into clerical dress; he stopped the dispensations, which were becoming so common as to be anticipated with confidence by married clergy converting to Catholicism. The twentieth-century Pope was forcing the Church back into the Middle Ages. The press became hostile.

In 1982 I made a film about the situation which forced me to face squarely the problem of authority in the Catholic Church. The basis of that authority is its consistency. The Church claims to have been founded by Christ to preserve and teach the deposit of faith which he bequeathed to it. The Supreme Teacher is the Pope, whose task it is to act as a final court of appeal against false interpretations of the faith. In this work he is guided by the Holy Spirit. And the Church proclaims that when the Pope, speaking from the seat of St Peter as Supreme Teacher, makes a pronouncement to the whole Church on a matter of faith or morals the Holy Spirit will not let him make a mistake. This is what the Catholic Church means when it claims that the Pope is infallible. It is a circumscribed infallibility, and critics have not been slow to point out that a second infallible authority may well be needed to judge which pronouncements are infallible. But this seems to me a flippant objection. Infallibility, after all, makes sense in the context of the Church's teaching authority. If the Pope is the guardian of divine truth he can hardly be anything else but protected from error.

His powers are celebrated in the golden letters that encircle the dome of St Peter's: TU ES PETRUS ET SUPER HANC PETRAM AEDIFICABO ECCLESIAM MEAM. The high drama of their position at the centre of the Catholic world is inescapably moving. And the words which follow, in the sixteenth chapter of St Matthew, seem even more specifically to locate authority in St Peter. They are translated, in the authorized version, 'I will give unto thee the keys of the kingdom of heaven: and whatsoever thou shalt bind on earth shall be bound in heaven: and whatsoever thou shalt loose on earth shall be loosed in heaven.' From this text, which, as we shall see later, has been loosely translated from the Greek, comes the papal emblem of the crossed keys and the widespread belief that the Pope, as vicar of St Peter, has full authority to bind and loose. The pope elected may well be the wrong man for the job. Although the cardinals pray for the guidance of the Holy Spirit when choosing him, there is no guarantee that they receive it, and there are some well-known historical personalities whose election to the office can hardly have been divinely inspired. But, once elected, the infallibility in teaching is conferred on the man sitting in the seat of St Peter no matter what his personal shortcomings may be.

It seemed to me, as I again studied this claim closely to make the film, that the Catholic Church finally fails to convince on this matter. The inconsistencies are inescapable. I had first noted them down in a school exercise book twenty years earlier. In the papal bull *Unam Sanctam* of 1302, Boniface VII stated, 'We declare, announce, and define that it is altogether necessary to salvation for every human creature to be subject to the Roman pontiff. The Lateran, Nov. 14 in our 8th year. As a perpetual memorial of this matter.' Nothing could more unequivocally express a teaching and a papal intention that it should be perpetually and universally binding. It was proclaimed by the Catholic Church for a thousand years. In 1863 in *Quanto Conficiamur,* Pius IX reminded the faithful, 'It is known that Catholic dogma states that nobody outside of the Catholic Church can be saved and that those who defy the authority of the Church . . . and the successor of St Peter, the Roman pontiff, to whom the custody of the vineyard was committed by the Saviour (as the Council of Chalcedon says), cannot gain eternal life.' Today this doctrine is denied by the Church and when, in the 1950s, the Jesuit Father Feeney with a group of Catholics in Boston taught it, the Holy Office intervened and declared all those to be excommunicate and *extra ecclesiam* (outside the Church) who maintained that *extra ecclesiam* nobody could be saved.

More recently, the attempt by the Pope to put an end to dissension over the ordination of women showed that infallibility, far from strengthening the Church's doctrinal position, weakens it. The Pope's decision on 'the inadmissibility of women to the ministerial priesthood' was not only framed as an infallible statement but was later declared by the Congregation for the Doctrine of the Faith to have been 'set forth infallibly by the ordinary and universal magisterium'. But it provoked widespread opposition in the press and a judgement from the Norris-Hulse Professor of Divinity at Cambridge University that 'The attempt to use the doctrine of infallibility, a doctrine intended to indicate the grounds and character of Catholic confidence in official teaching, as a blunt instrument to prevent the ripening of the question in the Catholic mind is a quite scandalous abuse of power, the most likely consequence of which will be further to undermine the authority which the Pope seeks to sustain.'

Now I had always been attracted to the Roman Catholic Church because of its apparent authority. I prefer to have my teeth drilled by a qualified dentist, my burst pipes fixed by a qualified plumber and my theological questions answered by a qualified theologian. The massive substructure of scholarship that underpins the doctrinal statements of the Pope had always seemed to me a reassuring backup to the claims of the Church to have been founded and protected from error by God. But when the authority of the Church is shown to be tenuously based and inconsistently exercised it ceases to carry weight. John Paul II struck me as a just, intelligent, holy man, compassionate and humanitarian. But he is not free, as Pope, to voice personal opinions about issues on which the Church has officially pronounced. The claim to authority has to be supported by consistency, since an organization which claims to be protected from error can hardly change its mind. The noble attempts of Pope John Paul II to bring the post-Vatican-II Roman Catholic Church back to its traditional teaching finally convinced me that the Church's claims to consistency were spurious.

At Oxford, Newman's superb *Essay on the Development of Christian Doctrine* had won me over to the view that a deposit of faith had been guarded by the Church and merely reinterpreted, with the guidance of the Holy Spirit, for succeeding generations. I should have been more cautious in exposing myself to the arguments of a stylist so persuasive that he could convince himself and many others (in Tract 90) that the Thirty-nine Articles, framed to define and justify the separation from Rome, were acceptable to Roman Catholics. As I lost confidence in the claims of the Roman Catholics, I had to abandon the search for a rational objective authority in religious matters.

At the same time as I finally gave up my hopes for the Catholic Church as a repository of the truth, I came across a striking man who had journeyed in the opposite direction. In the summer of 1984 I wrote and presented a programme about the German economist Fritz Schumacher, then famous as the author of a best-selling book *Small is Beautiful*, published in Britain in 1973. His book was an analysis of the economic structure of Western civilization by an academic economist, and as such was, to me, unpromising material. But Schumacher had pointed out in lively prose that the pursuit of profit in the West had led to the growth of giant organizations which were increasingly specialized, and this in turn had led to gross inefficiency, environmental pollution and inhumane working conditions. This was a message in touch with the spirit of the times.

It was taken up by the self-sufficiency lobby, along with Gandhian ideas about carding and spinning our own jumpers, and seemed unlikely to be more than a passing fad, but I found to my surprise that *Small is Beautiful* is filled with stimulating notions even for a reader for whom economics is a foreign country. Early in the book, Schumacher quotes Keynes's counselling that economic progress is obtainable only if we employ those powerful drives of human selfishness which religion and traditional wisdom universally call upon us to resist. On the way to economic prosperity, Keynes had written, 'We must pretend to ourselves and to everyone that fair is foul and foul is fair; for foul is useful and fair is not. Avarice and usury and precaution must be our gods for a little longer still.'

Clearly, Schumacher was much more than an economist, and I read with delight the biography of him written by Barbara Wood, one of his daughters, before spending some time with her and recording a long interview.

He had been an extreme intellectual in his youth, a quintessential rationalist. The brain ruled. On his marriage night he insisted on separate beds, because he had observed that the eldest child in a family was often the most difficult character and put this down to the fact that it was often conceived on the wedding night when the couple were excited and inebriated. He wouldn't take the risk.

He believed in the high ideals of Western culture and accepted that they may have been derived from Christianity, although the religion itself would not stand up to rational investigation. He wrote that '... man, *en masse*, is determined by material factors of his environment. Do not wait for the spiritual revolution. Change the environment.' And he often quoted Brecht's phrase *'Erst kommt das Fressen, dann kommt die Moral'* – 'First comes the belly, then comes morality.' He saw religion as speculation, wishful thinking unsupported by facts, and rejected it as simply untrue. His rejection was forceful:

Science is the organized attempt of mankind to discover how things work as a causal system. Since everything has a cause, the realm of science is everything ... I further hold that it is unworthy of thinking men to succumb to their *horror vacui* in the field of knowledge and understanding and to give answers to unsolved problems 'by act of faith' merely because they should like to have an answer. The smallest item of observational knowledge appeals more to my aesthetic, yes, also to my moral, sense than the most glorious superstructure built by statements unsupported by or in contradiction with facts.

His change of heart was brought about by British Rail. The train journey between Caterham, where he lived, and Victoria, the station for the headquarters of the National

Coal Board, where he worked, took forty minutes each way.
English people do not talk to each other on trains; they read
aggressively to avoid human contact. Schumacher decided to
spend the travelling time increasing his knowledge of world
cultures. He began to study the ancient civilizations of the
East, and found that to understand them he had to read
about their religions. He was struck by a passage in
Radhakrishnan:

> The present crisis in human affairs is due to a profound crisis
> in human consciousness, a lapse from the organic wholeness
> of life. There is a tendency to overlook the spiritual and exalt
> the intellectual . . . The business of the intellectual is to dispel
> the mystery, put an end to dreams, strip life of its illusions,
> and reduce the great play of human life to a dull show, comic
> on occasions but tragic more frequently.

Perhaps it was the phrase 'organic wholeness' that caught his
imagination. He wrote to his parents:

> Through this contact with Indian and Chinese philosophy
> and religion my whole way of thinking has come into motion.
> New possibilities of knowledge (and experience) have been
> opened to me of whose existence I had no inkling. I feel as
> men during the Renaissance must have felt. All the conclu-
> sions I had come to have to be thought through again.

The result of this thinking through was that he became, for a
time, a Buddhist and, after many years of reading and
analysis, was received into the Roman Catholic Church in
1971.

In 1977 he wrote a small book outlining his philosophy in
which I was struck by two coincidences between his spiritual
journey and my own. He told the story of being shown a map
of Leningrad when on a visit there and asking an interpreter
why the churches which he could see in the city were not
marked on the map. The interpreter explained that 'living
churches' – that is, the ones used for worship – were not

shown, only the churches set up as museums. And he realized that all through school and university he had been given maps of life which left out its most important features:

> The maps I was given advised me that virtually all my ancestors, until a quite recent generation, had been rather pathetic illusionists who conducted their lives on the basis of irrational beliefs and absurd superstitions. Even illustrious scientists like Johann Kepler or Isaac Newton apparently spent most of their time and energy on nonsensical studies of non-existing beings ... The maps of *real* knowledge designed for *real* life did not show anything except things that allegedly could be *proved* to exist.

Yes, I remembered consulting the same maps at school in my textbooks and encyclopaedias.

He went on to claim that the maps produced by modern materialistic scientism leave out all the questions that really matter. And he quoted with approval a dictum of St Thomas Aquinas that reversed his previous conviction: 'the slenderest knowledge that may be obtained of the highest things is more desirable than the most certain knowledge obtained of lesser things'.

His quotation of Aquinas was the second coincidence which attracted me to Schumacher to my advantage. I had studied the *Summa* in Fiji, and on the title-page of my first book, *The Charter of the Land: Custom and Colonisation in Fiji*, I had quoted:

> The savage of Fiji broke beyond the common limits of rapine and bloodshed and ... stood unrivalled as a disgrace to mankind. (William Calvert, *Mission History*).

> Their disposition is mild and generous towards their friends and the affection they bear towards their relatives is seldom found among Europeans' (*The Journal of a Sandal wood Trader*).

'Cognitum autem est in cognoscente secundum modum
cognoscentis'
(St Thomas Aquinas, S. T. 1, Q.12. a.4,c).

By this last quotation I meant no more than to suggest that
what people saw in an exotic society depended on the
prejudices they brought to the observation. Schumacher had
used the same quotation, but expanded its significance into a
crucially important principle: that of Adequatio. This states
simply that we can know only those things we are capable of
knowing. We each have a capacity for knowledge, and if we
are presented with a reality which exceeds that capacity we
shall not recognize it as reality. He uses musical sensitivity as
an example, and points out that individuals can vary from
those who can grasp the content and meaning of an entire
symphony from one hearing or reading of the score to those
who cannot absorb it at all no matter how often they hear it.
For the former the symphony is as real as it was to the
composer; for the latter there is no symphony, only a series of
meaningless noises. Schumacher deduced from this that we
are not entitled to insist that something inaccessible to us has
no existence.

All this seemed to me at the time to make good sense, but I
had to maintain that, if I was inadequate when it came to
religious truth, it was not for want of honest investigation. I
was examining the claims of believers in every film that we
made, and I found them unconvincing. The Christian Church
taught that I could not fully understand its gospel without
grace. I had not been given grace, and found it puzzling that
someone who had been searching for so long and so
assiduously should be denied a commodity which is freely
given. I should repeat that I would never have used the word
'searching', since that could imply a need to discover. I was
always consistently wary of acknowledging a *need*, because
any truth which answers a need can be put down to self-
deception. If I were ever to discover religious truth, it had to
be from a position of security and happiness – the truth that

comes to someone with a good digestion, an adequate income, a happy marriage, a full life and excellent health.

Apart from the intense and largely cerebral investigations into the claims of different religions, many of which left a deposit of awareness in a mind which rejected their larger claims, I was influenced during the *Everyman* years at a more subtle and profound level by meeting and talking intimately with a number of good people. By this I mean people who seem to defy the psychological and biological explanations of how human beings work. Such people have always seemed to me to pose a problem far more intractable than the problem of evil. That evil should exist in a world populated by beings with free will whose actions are influenced by feelings of insecurity, resentment and self-interest has never seemed at all difficult to explain. But how do we account for motiveless goodness: acts which seem to be spontaneous, self-sacrificing and focused on promoting the well-being of somebody else? These sit uneasily in the reductionist biologist view of humanity, though attempts have been made to explain them in terms of the preservation of gene pools. I had known one person whose life seemed to be unaccountably and entirely devoted to other people's well-being: Ada Hopper, my Sunday-school teacher. I was to meet others.

The first was Catherine Bramwell Booth, ninety-four years old when I met her in 1976, granddaughter of William Booth, founder of the Salvation Army. I had been warned that she was eccentric and could be a difficult person to interview as she 'didn't suffer fools gladly' – a phrase that is often applied to the self-centredly pompous. When we met, she shook hands vigorously and swept the small group with a radiant smile: cameraman, sound man, researcher, producer and me. 'Now', she said. 'I am going to pray. We need help in what we are about to do, and I shall ask God for it. You may not believe that he is listening, but fortunately that does not depend on you and I know he is here with us.' She closed her eyes, folded her hands, and asked in a simple prayer that we might all be helped. Then she sat down and composed herself for the questions. I do not remember in detail what we discussed, but I expect I challenged her about the relevance of the Salvation Army with its 'blood and fire' approach in the modern liberal and secular world, as well as digging gently at the certainties which seemed to animate her world. She replied brightly, firmly and with complete conviction. At the end of the interview I asked her, not without a touch of impudence, whether, at the age of ninety-four, she was now looking forward to meeting Jesus, who had so intimately ruled her life. 'If you mean am I keen to die,' she replied, 'of course not. I love life. Every morning I wake with delight at the prospect of another day. I can't have too many of them. I know that I shall be with Jesus when I die, but I'm in no hurry.'

Another good person I met was David Sheppard, Bishop of Liverpool. I went there in 1975 to film him and conduct a long interview on his appointment to the diocese. He had written a book, published the previous year, called *Built as a City: God and the Urban World Today*, in which he dealt with the problem of bringing the Christian message to the poor. It contained insightful comments about the relationship between the classes in Britain. He had noted that the working-classes tend to think of the Church (of England) as a middle-class institution and that the process of conversion to Christianity involves a crash course in middle-class morals. I was impressed by the insights, but, as a product of the working-class, I doubted his capacity to conceive them. After all, David Sheppard had led a privileged life: public school, then Cambridge University, playing cricket for his county, for Cambridge and then for England. His comfortable middle-class background, national celebrity as a sportsman and film-star looks had clearly insulated him against life as we knew it in the working-classes. What could he know of deprivation? How had he the brass neck to expound on suffering?

Of course I was coming at him at an angle, bent askew by the chip on my shoulder. But I saw David Sheppard as the

Arthur Winnington-Ingram of our times. Dear old A. W.-I. had been Bishop of London from 1901 to 1939. In spite of coming from one of the leading families in Worcestershire, brought up to shooting and fishing, educated at Marlborough public school and Oxford University, Winnington-Ingram tried to identify himself with the London poor by affecting a cockney accent. He was a dapper man who shaved twice a day and bathed three times. This latter practice he never failed to recommend to the poor at public meetings, even though few of them had ever seen a bath. 'After my bath', he claimed one day, 'I step out and feel rosy all over.' Voice from the back: 'Who's Rosie?'

When I met David Sheppard I liked him and wanted him to be at ease on camera, so I told him the line of questioning I had in mind to pursue. He thought for a while and then asked if I would go to breakfast with him and his wife, Grace, before the interview, which was scheduled for next day. We chatted about general things over breakfast, and I told him about my background and my interest in religious questions. After we had eaten, Grace poured fresh cups of coffee and said to David, 'Shall we tell him?' He nodded, and so she then told me something of their life together. It had not been easy, particularly since he was made bishop, because she was agoraphobic and panicked in company. I immediately identified with this. She had not been sure whether to tell me until they had both decided that I could be trusted with the information. She told me that David had decided to refuse promotion in the Church because of the strain under which she would be put, and had changed his mind only after long and agonizing discussions together. They were a devoted and close couple, and he wanted above all things to protect her from strain. She asked whether it would help give a more rounded portrait of David if she were to speak about this on television.

And then she went on to tell me about her cancer. It had shown itself suddenly some years before. There had been a time when the prognosis was bad, and it seemed that the rest of their time together would be brief and painful. David Sheppard had then known suffering as I could not imagine it. Then the cancer went into remission. Both recovered and went on to face life with that apparent easy self-confidence and good humour which I had stupidly thought could only be the product of a sheltered existence. I had met good people again, and felt reprimanded.

There was also Trevor Huddleston, with the ascetic manner, penetrating gaze and wonderful voice, pacing through the graveyard at the Community of the Resurrection in Mirfield and showing me the spot where he hoped his body would lie. Of course he had international celebrity, and it was possible to see his work in South Africa as courting this, but five minutes in his company made you realize the passionate commitment to something outside himself and the true humility that springs from such a commitment.

Mirfield also introduced me to Hugh Bishop, who became a close friend. He had been Superior of the Community for many years, but had resigned because its rules forbade individual relationships. The brothers were enjoined to love each other, but only as a community. Hugh felt that Christian love need not and perhaps should not be simply an unfocused feeling of generalized benevolence. He had the need to express his love for an individual, and so he left, causing a scandal. He hoped, as did I, that by explaining himself on television he would diminish the scandal and increase understanding of the situation. I am not sure that we were right, but making the film allowed me to meet a man I came to value highly as sensitive and intelligent, with an almost total forgetfulness of self that made him keenly interested and concerned with the well-being of others. He was a good man.

The final series I did for *Everyman* was, I thought at the time, the end of a long journey. I hoped it might have some value for people interested in contemporary Christianity, because it sought to find out exactly what a 'Christian' is. *The Shorter*

Oxford Dictionary records that since the sixteenth century the word has meant, colloquially, 'a decent, respectable, or presentable person', and *The Oxford Dictionary of the Christian Church* notes that the name 'Christian' 'has tended, in nominally Christian countries, to lose any credal significance and imply only that which is ethically praiseworthy or socially customary'. Crossing the Atlantic to that great country which speaks the world's most widely used version of English, I found in the *American Thesaurus of Slang* the following synonyms for 'Christian': 'white, respectable, good egg, regular, square toes, steady man'.

So had we reached a stage when Christianity meant no more than respectability? This seemed undeniable in the usage of the secular age, though it would have been hotly contested, I remembered, by members of the Humanist Association, who were always and rightly impatient with the assumption that the only respectable people were Christians.

A simple and obvious way of describing a Christian, which would have applied through most of the centuries before our own would be someone who holds that the Christian Creed is true. For almost 2,000 years the great certainties of the Christian faith were celebrated at the heart of the worship of the Church, as they stand at the centre of Bach's B-minor Mass. These were the revealed truths that had stood firm against all the divisions of Christendom. It was simply the capacity to assent to them that made a person a Christian. But in our own time we had seen bishops of the Church, whose duty it is to guide the faithful in Christian truth, publicly denying credal statements such as the virgin birth and the resurrection of Christ. The accepted attitude among liberal theologians is that the Creeds were drawn up in an age of heresy and are no longer central to Christian faith; that their language is symbolic and needs to be interpreted for each age. But such teachings had been accused by Reinhold Niebuhr of leading to a Christianity in which 'a God without wrath has brought a man without sin, through a Christ without a cross, to a Kingdom without judgement'.

For ten years I had been trying to discover a definable content to contemporary Christian belief. I had developed the habit of asking clergymen, theologians and lay apologists what they felt was the irreducible minimum of faith which a person must possess to be properly called a Christian. They all agreed that the question was a fascinating one, and then went on to talk about something else.

I thought I had a way of concentrating their minds. All the Churches have ways of instructing catechumens who seek admission and of examining them as to the content and correctness of what they believe before letting them in. At the point of entry, surely, the distinction must be established between who is a Christian and who is not. So I would approach each of the established Churches as a postulant seeking admission and find out what I had to believe to get in. This, surely, would represent the irreducible minimum I was looking for and would define what Christianity meant to the church I was seeking to enter. The mini-series, in two parts, was called 'Can I Come In?'

All of the mainstream churches shrank from insisting on the Creed as an entry qualification. They suggested that subscription to its articles might come towards the end, and not at the beginning of a Christian life. This surprised me, since the Creed was included in all the major catechisms. Church leaders admitted that if their clergy asked for too much, candidates might not come forward. When I pressed them to set out for me the irreducible minimum of faith which makes a person a Christian, they were evasive.

The Anglican said it is sufficient to want to be a follower of Jesus Christ; the Methodist said that the the central doctrine of his church was difficult to define but, 'in one way or another you must make reference to Jesus Christ' and 'in one way or another you must refer to the possibility of forgiveness'. The Presbyterian was more demanding, saying that the irreducible minimum was 'a clear recognition of a Trinitarian Church' and that he would ask any candidate for admission: 'Do you believe in God as your Heavenly Father? In Christ as your Saviour and Lord? And in the Holy Spirit as your Sanctifier?' The Baptist stressed the necessity of a conversion experience and admitted a distaste for creeds, ending with the statement 'We do not bind the conscience of individuals to a form of words'. The Roman Catholic admitted that his church, having been around longest, had the largest body of doctrine, and said that, to become a Catholic it was necessary to believe the doctrines of the church. But then he went on to say 'I don't think people should be refused entry to the church because they are not capable of assenting to everything explicitly.'

I had opened the series at a cricket ground, dressed in whites, padded up and waiting to go in to bat. I reminded viewers of the essentially English attitude to Christianity immortalized in the quatrain:

> For when the One Great Scorer comes
> To write against your name,
> He marks – not that you won or lost –
> But how you played the game.

I said that I hoped to discover that Christianity had not been gentled down to a code of seemly behaviour, that it had a kernel of supernatural truth, and that I should discover from the leaders of the mainstream churches what that kernel was. At the end of the series I appeared again on the cricket field and spoke a little piece which reflected my state of mind at the time:

There seems to be general feeling abroad in the churches today that Christianity has more to do with a subjective relationship than with objective truth: that somehow if we can bring ourselves to feel that we are walking with Christ, we can forget about the Creeds.

Now, if this is so, it represents an important change of heart:

because for centuries the churches have taught that those

truths which a man was able to acknowedge and confess in this life affected his eternal destiny.

And if, in the interests of a common humanity, we have diminished those truths so as to bring closer together those people who are Christian and those who are not –

Then we may be able to play cricket together –
but I don't think we'll build many more churches.

Chapter Seven

My first contact with the Orthodox Church was on 4 May 1975. At midnight, the BBC was to broadcast the Easter liturgy from the Russian Orthodox Church in Ennismore Gardens, London, for the ears of the faithful in the Soviet Union. I was not directly involved in the broadcast, which was part of the BBC's Russian service, but one of the *Everyman* producers had raised the idea of a documentary about Orthodoxy, and I went along as reporter to observe.

Midnight has never been my best time of day. My bodily rhythms were shaped on a farm and have remained stubbornly agricultural, although I keep trying to bend them to fit in with my more sophisticated friends. On the few midnights which find me up and about, my biorhythms have been screaming at me for at least a couple of hours that, according to natural law, I should be in bed. They were specially insistent, I remember, on the night of 4 May 1975 because I had been up since four a.m. to present the *Sunday* programme on Radio 4. So I was in poor shape for a life-transforming experience.

The images were unforgettable. Into the total darkness of a silent church a solitary candle flame appeared. Three candles were burning with a single light. Behind it was a bearded face, a hint of eyes and teeth, then flashes from brilliant points of light – red, blue, green and a dazzling white – as the jewels encrusting cloaks, crosses, mitres, books came alive into the blackness. Then another candle was lit from those first, three from the second, twenty from them, and the flames spread all through the priests and people with a great shout: 'Christ is risen!' Hundreds of candle flames lit the faces of the people and threw light up on to the great iconostasis from which Christ, his mother and the saints looked down – dark, penetrating eyes set in faces that seemed all gold and green. The splendour was compelling. The choir burst into a swelling hymn of joy rich with Russian harmonies over an unbelievably deep bass that made the toes tingle.

When, towards the end of the tenth century, Prince Vladimir of Kiev decided that his people needed a religion, so the story goes, he sent out emissaries to all the religious centres of the world to report on which of the ones practised at the time seemed most suitable for Russia. The emissaries were unimpressed by the Western Christianity they found in Germany, which was no doubt a little regimented for their tastes; they decided that Judaism would not suit the Russian temperament, and they rejected Islam as soon as they heard of the prohibition on alcohol. At Constantinople they attended a service in Agia Sophia and reported enthusiastically to their master:

> We knew not whether we were in heaven or on earth, for surely there is no such splendour or beauty anywhere upon earth. We cannot describe it to you; only this we know, that God dwells there among men and that their service surpasses the worship of all other places. For we cannot forget that beauty . . .

Vladimir was converted, and with him Kievan Russia. The liturgy which I experienced that night in London was the same as that seen by his emissaries, as enriched by a thousand years of Russian culture. It was undeniably splendid, and would make magnificent television, but I wondered, as I at last found my bed in the early hours, what it had to do with the simplicity of New Testament Christianity.

For much of the summer of 1975 we worked on the

Orthodox film. I read all the books I could find on the history and teachings of the Orthodox Church, and was surprised to discover that what I had taken to be an institution set up and nurtured by the tsars of Russia to keep the peasants loyal laid claim to deeper roots. The Orthodox Church – Greek and Russian – saw itself as the Original Church, founded by Christ, against which the gates of hell would not prevail; which had never been split by reformation or remoulded by counter-reformation; which had been untouched by the destructive forces of Western rationalism; which had preserved and taught 'Orthodoxy', literally 'Right teaching'. Far from thinking of itself as having broken away from the Catholic Church, it claimed that the Roman Catholics had broken away from it. And I was delighted to find that the Orthodox thought of the Pope in Rome as the leader of the Protestant world.

The choirmaster at Ennismore Gardens, Father Michael Fortounatto, helped me in my researches by answering questions, explaining points of liturgy, teaching and history, and lending me books. He was not only a fine musician, who directed the choir in a series of magnificent recordings of Orthodox music, but a scholar who spoke fluent English, Russian and French and was well up in the modern French philosophers, especially the materialists, a kindly father confessor to the community and a man who combined in his life to an extreme degree unflagging enthusiasm and total exhaustion.

During the making of the film I came to realize two things about the Orthodox Church: that its historic claims to continuity were persuasive and that its appeal to the senses was impressive. I think I would have said at the time that, if any existing branch of the Christian Church had preserved a truth, this was, in purely rational historical forms, the most likely; and that in purely sensual terms – the stimulation of eyes, nose and ears – the Russian Orthodox liturgy came tops.

And I noticed something else, which seemed trivial at the

time but was to prove decisive: the Russian Orthodox Christians I met had an enormous appetite for life which seemed to turn 'Christianity' on its head. Within English culture, the term 'Christian' has, as we have seen, connotations of seemliness, moderation and propriety. The model English Christians are constantly aware of the need to guard against the sins of the flesh, and sometimes do so by being embarrassed by their appetites. They try not to ask for second helpings, and always try to get up from the table feeling they could eat a little more. It was in England that the words were penned 'Thou hast conquered, O pale Galilean; the world has grown grey from Thy breath.'

But these Russian Christians ate and drank hugely, and then burst into song and would roar all night given half a chance. They were excessive in everything. They laughed and wept and shouted and kissed each other. They were passionate about music, painting, poetry, conversation. And when I asked them if all this zest for living was the triumph of Russianness over Christianity they protested that, on the cóntrary, the zest was the essence of their Christianity. Since God became incarnate and transformed the material world, matter could henceforth be spirit-bearing; things of the flesh were to be enjoyed as part of the worship of God. 'We are an incarnational faith!' they would shout, uncorking a bottle. 'We are a Trinitarian faith!' they would cry as they opened the third. I was not convinced of the theology behind it all, but I certainly approved of its effects.

For the next few years I was too busy looking into religious stories from other faiths in different parts of the world to keep up my researches into Orthodoxy. And then something happened in our private life which jolted us into a change of direction. Felicia had been unwell for some time, and as the symptoms worsened we went to see a consultant neurologist who diagnosed multiple sclerosis. He would make no predictions as to the likely course of the disease, but we learned enough to realize that there would be a deterioration of functions and a reduced probability of old age. Felicia decided that, if the amount of time she had left was to be reduced, then it should be improved in quality. Unlike me, she was aware of a spiritual dimension in her life and wanted to explore this further. As she is the most intensely visual person I know, I suggested a faith with a rich tradition of icon painting and one which seemed, more than any I had met, to enhance the quality of life. I introduced her to Father Michael Fortounatto.

After only a few months of conversations with Father Michael, Felicia, who has a temperamental aversion to delay of any kind, came to a decision and was baptized. From that time, early 1983, she attended weekly services every Sunday morning at the Russian Orthodox Church in Devon. Often I would go with her, but spend the time she was in church sitting in the car reading. Because she was following an Orthodox path, I wanted to understand where it might be leading her, and so in my usual way I tried to find the answers in books. Fortunately, books were available in plenty because the deacon of the church was on the staff of the Russian department at Exeter University and was generous in recommending and lending them.

It was the first time I had met Russian theology and philosophy. The combination, confronted for a couple of hours every week in the back seat of a car, gradually undermined the basic intellectual presuppositions I had come to accept in the previous forty years. It may help to summarize them now. I had come to accept that the highest cognitived faculty we possess is our reason. All human experience, however powerful, however mystical, has to be brought to the bar of the reason to be properly evaluated. This is not to deny the authority of subjective experiences which cannot be expressed in words or be understood by the reason, but such experiences have authority only for the person who has them. They are interesting but unpersuasive for the rest of us.

Theology is the attempt by the human reason to explain

God. The supreme theologians, it had seemed to me, were the scholastics of the Roman Catholic Church, who accept the basic premiss that the unaided human reason can arrive at an awareness of the existence of God and an understanding of his works. I had assembled a large collection of books on theology which I mentally divided into those which explained ultimate realities using lucid and rational language and those (which I called the 'ineffables') which claimed that religion was inexpressible and then went on trying to express it. Broadly, the rational ones were from the Roman or Anglican Churches and the 'ineffables' from the extreme Protestant. The intellectual snob in me noted that the books which protested most against the powers of the human reason were written by people whose rational faculty appeared to be least developed.

The Russians undermined all this. First came Vladimir Lossky with his *The Mystical Theology of the Eastern Church*, explaining with perfect lucidity that, since the matters with which theology concerns itself are ultimately mystical, all theology has to be based in mysticism if it is to contain the truth, just as all mysticism must be theologically structured if it is to be authoritative and communicable. The theology of the Orthodox Church, he points out, is apophatic: that is, it seeks to explain God, not by making positive statements about him, since these must be untrue, but by negations. If we say that God is good, compassionate, merciful etc., then these statements are inadequate if judged by human standards – the only ones we know. Similarly if we say that God exists, this is untrue if we mean by it that he is an existent object among many. So we can come closer to the truth by saying what God is not. This approach to God is, of course, older than the Orthodox Church, older than Christianity, since I remembered the Upanishads speaking of the Brahman as *neti, neti* – 'not this, not this'. It was clear from every page of *The Mystical Theology of the Eastern Church* that the author's rational faculty was well developed. His mind was well stocked, his prose that of a practised intellectual. And yet his message seemed to put him with the 'ineffables'. He was using his rational faculty to give ultimate authority to mysticism. The Russians were going to be difficult to classify.

Most interesting were the writers who had gone through a phase of intellectual rationalism and come out the other side into Orthodoxy. Since I had come to accept that the natural evolution of human thought led in the opposite direction, I was curious to follow their arguments. One of the most colourful was Ivan Kireyevsky (1806–56), who was born into a highly cultured Moscow family with a father who was a Freemason and dabbled in Enlightenment thought and a mother who was prominent in the literary salons of the time. He was educated privately by tutors who excited him with the latest ideas of the German philosophical schools and then sent him to Berlin to hear Hegel, Ritter and Schliermacher, then on to Munich, where his brother Peter was studying with Schelling. Ivan returned to Russia with a mission to propagate Western philosophical ideas there. He had met both Hegel and Schelling, was convinced of the importance of their philosophy, and was deeply scornful of the Orthodox teachings of the established Church. His first article, called 'The Nineteenth Century', written for a journal he founded himself, expressed these ideas forcefully; the journal was suppressed by the censors because of it. He narrowly escaped being imprisoned.

Kireyevsky then spent a couple of years in Moscow, trying to publish his Western progressive ideas and to find a place on the staff of the university. He failed in both ambitions and decided to settle down with a devout wife and run his country estate. The twin influences of the estate and the wife seem to have brought about a sea change in his ideas. His property was close to the monastery of Optina Pustin, and he met there the spiritual fathers who were to have such an influence on Dostoevsky and Tolstoy. He even built on his estate a wooden hut for one of them, Macarius, to retreat to occasionally, and under his influence he began to study Greek patristic literature. This amazed him. He said he found in the Greek Fathers all that was most important and true in Schelling's philosophy, developed more fully and stated more exactly. He underwent a complete conversion to Orthodoxy and became the philosopher of the Slavophile movement.

What most impressed me at first in Kireyevsky's writing was his analysis of what had gone wrong with Western Christianity and Western philosophy. Under the influence of Aristotle and its most brilliant scholastic theologians, the Western Church, he wrote, had erected a system of legalistic dogma which went far beyond Christian traditions. This meant that it could no longer claim the authority of tradition, and so had to locate authority in the hierarchy of the Church itself. The Protestant Reformation, rejecting that authority, had replaced it by Scripture, which, being individually interpreted, had led to the splintering of the Protestants into a thousand sects and finally to the rejection of faith. Russia had escaped the rationalism and juridicism which the spirit of Ancient Rome, through the papacy, had imposed on the Christian Church, and so Orthodoxy was free from the legalism of Rome and had escaped that rebellion against it which had caused the Reformation. There seemed to me to be a high degree of probability in this argument, though I realized that Kireyevsky was selective in his analysis: he based his argument on the Russian Church at its best, and ignored the abuses which had chequered its history.

As for Western philosophy, he again identified Aristotle as the destructive force, because it was he who located the instrument for the search for truth in the human reason. The acceptance of this error had forced Western philosophers into an impotent rationalism which could locate truth only in the concatenations of logical argument and abstract thought. Kireyevsky proposed an idea of what he called 'integral cognition', including the realms of feeling, desire and intention which put a person into contact with reality and with other people before any process of abstract thinking. We can be saved from the errors of logical thought only when we keep the exercise of 'reason' under the control of this 'integral cognition', which is the fundamental cognitive relationship of humanity to reality.

For somebody who has accepted all that human experience should be brought to the bar of reason to be properly assessed, the notion that reason itself should be assessed elsewhere seemed faintly dotty. But Kireyevsky's argument is persuasive. He does not exchange reason for some other faculty, but proposes to use it in conjunction with other faculties:

> The first condition for the elevation of reason is that man should strive to gather into one indivisible whole all his separate forces, which in the ordinary condition of man are in a state of incompleteness and contradiction; that he should not consider his abstract logical capacity as the only organ for the comprehension of truth; that he should not consider the voice of enraptured feeling uncoordinated with other forces of the spirit as the faultless guide to truth; that he should not consider the promptings of an isolated aesthetic sense, independent of other concepts, as a true guide to the comprehension of the higher organization of the universe; that he should not consider even the dominant love of his heart, separate from the other demands of the spirit, as the infallible guide to the attainment of the supreme good; but that he should constantly seek in the depth of his soul that inner root of understanding where all the separate forces merge into one living and whole vision of the mind.

I am quite sure that, sitting in my car on a Sunday morning and reading those words, I did not feel persuaded by the whole argument. And I know I must have felt sceptical about the existence of the 'inner root of understanding'. But Kireyevsky challenged, it seemed to me effectively, the primacy of reason as the cognitive faculty. His arguments put me in mind of Radhakrishnan; how often Orthodoxy seemed expressible in the terms of Hinduism:

Simply because a [mystical insight] is incommunicable, it does not become less valid than other forms of knowledge. We can describe this experience only by metaphors . . . intellect need not be negated, but has only to be supplemented. A philosophy based on intuition is not necessarily opposed to reason and understanding. Intuition can throw light on the dark places which intellect is unable to penetrate. The results of mystical intuition require to be subjected to logical analysis. And it is only by this process of mutual correction and supplementation that each can live a sober life . . . The ideal of the intellect is realized in the intuitive experience, for in the supreme are all contradictories reconciled.

In the late spring of 1983 I went to Russia to make a television documentary about the freedom of the press and how responsible Russian journalists coped without it. We focused on the deputy editor of *Izvestia*, because he had been a diplomat in New York and London, spoke excellent English, and was able to compare and contrast the Soviet and Western systems. His attitude was that the Western insistence on the universality of a particular value, namely the freedom of the press, which had evolved over a long period in the development of Western societies, was a form of cultural imperialism. The press, he claimed, was an agent for nation-building, for the promotion of national consciousness. The establishment of a national identity must override individual rights. The Western press he saw as perpetuating a destructively inegalitarian system. He took me into an outer office in the *Izvesia* building where all the British Sundays were spread out on a large table. With a sweeping gesture across the banner headlines proclaiming their usual weekly litany of sex and sleaze, he asked, 'Can you really be proud in the West of what you do with your so-called freedom?' I could not.

The successful journalist in the Soviet Union at the time had power, money, and privileges which, it seemed to me, sat uneasily with the aims of Article 19 of the Constitution of the USSR for 'social homogeneity . . . the elimination of class distinctions and of the essential differences between mental and physical labour'. The explanation, which I was to hear many times from those who enjoyed wealth and privilege under the Soviet system, was that these differences in status were temporary aberrations in a nation on the march towards the goal of communism. They were tolerated as emergency measures to be rejected when the goal was achieved. Since the rate of progress towards it was governed by social elites who stood to lose their status on arrival, delays and inefficiencies were understandable.

These considerations were incidental to my own journey, which on the evening we arrived, took me to the famous multicoloured onion-domed Cathedral of St Basil to experience Russian Orthodoxy close to the roots. The interior was disappointing, with lots of gilt and sentimentality and an exhibition of coats of chain mail and battleaxes. I soon left and crossed to the Kremlin, to the splendours of the Cathedral of the Annunciation, for long the private chapel of the ruling dynasty in Russia. The icons, by Theophilus the Greek and Andrei Rublev, were stunning in their simplicity and beautifully set off by the red-brown jasper floor, a gift from the Shah of Persia. But this was on show as a museum and art gallery; groups of tourists jostled with each other as guides intoned their recitals of historical facts in different languages. It was not an uplifting experience.

Hoping for a taste of Russian religion in practice, I got up next morning at six and took the metro to the Church of the Epiphany, in north Moscow, which I was told was open and functioning as the Moscow cathedral. It was a massive stone building, with enormous gaudy ultramarine doors on the front elevation and golden domes above. The doors were locked. The church was dark and silent. I walked round it a couple of times and then discovered a small side door which opened into an appalling interior. All the icons were modern sentimental Italianate copies in enormous gilt frames with glass to protect them from the kisses of the few old women in headscarves who bowed and crossed themselves, it seemed mechanically and interminably, in front of them. There were two little old men with completely bald heads who pushed the women away from time to time and blew out the candles as they burned low. The atmosphere seemed heavy with senility and superstition. Which is, I suppose, precisely what the authorities wanted it to be.

It seemed that all the Byzantine icons had been removed from the functioning churches and placed in art galleries. I had great hopes of enjoying the positive side of this cultural vandalism by seeing the magnificent collection housed together in the Tretyakov Gallery, but when I got there the curator congratulated me on arriving at a privileged time. All the icons had been shut away in the basement, and I could enjoy as a special treat an exhibition of Soviet Realistic painting featuring flaxen-haired girls with rippling muscles on tractors.

I left Russia with the feeling that I had had some direct contact with an authentic religious tradition, but only in the churches which were preserved as museums. There the icons were Byzantine and the atmosphere still bore traces of reverence. The functioning Orthodox Church seemed to service a tiny number of sentimental older people whose social function was to demonstrate the irrelevance of their faith to anyone sound in mind and body.

Back in England I kept up my Sundays sitting outside the church reading, until somebody – possibly the priest – suggested that I might learn more by the direct experience of attending the services. I had made one attempt at this. During a conversation with Metropolitan Anthony (Anthony Bloom) he had told me that the best approach to Orthodoxy was simply to attend the divine liturgy and be open to whatever happened. 'The service is long, by Western standards,' he had admitted, 'but even Orthodox services eventually come to an end. You should simply stand there and allow yourself to respond to whatever promptings you get.' So I had stood for an hour and a half one Sunday morning while the people around me were being religious: crossing themselves, saying prayers, reciting the Creed, queuing for communion. And I was bored. Their piety did not touch me. With Francis Galton peering over my shoulder, I found embarrassing their repeated litanies of prayers for the Queen, for seasonable weather and the abundance fruits of the earth, and for those who travel by water and by land. Only the music made the experience tolerable for me. A Russian choir singing church music could make standing in a supermarket queue enjoyable.

So when I was asked to join the choir, I saw a way of being present at the liturgy without tedium. They asked me not because I had any musical ability but because all men who sing in Russian choirs want to sing the bass part: that unbelievably rich, low, pulsating rumble that is the mark of Slavonic singing by Russian voices. The tenor part in small communities is often left to the women. I was able to have a go at it, so the choirmistress, relieved at being able to release a female voice to sing a female part, encouraged me to try. My sight-reading was weak, so I persuaded Father Michael Fortounatto, who happened to be staying with us one weekend, to sing the tenor part of the entire liturgy into a cassette recorder and I then played his recording to myself over and over again as I travelled in the car until I had it by heart. I was able to stay with the choir most of the time, though I had to fall silent when any variations on the part I had learned cropped up.

For the first year or so I spent my time in church with my eyes fixed on the face of the choirmistress, of whom I was mildly terrified. A flicker of pain indicated that I was singing too loudly or too soft; a spasm of agony as if somebody had thrust a bayonet into her entrails meant that I had gone off key. Occasionally – rarely – a beatific smile would spread across her face as we came to the end of a piece and she would give a curt nod. We had it right. I was far too unsure of myself during this time to give anything less than my complete attention to the singing, so I did not really notice what was going on around me. But after about a year I knew some of the liturgy well enough to allow my eyes to wander over the congregation occasionally, and I came to realize what a diverse bunch of people they were: quite a few locals; Russians and Greeks from the university; a couple of ex-Anglican priests; the cluster of white heads such as are to be found in any English church on any Sunday morning; young couples with children; a handful of students of indeterminate age, sex and nationality. And I began to wonder what had led all these very different people to Orthodoxy. So I decided to make a radio programme to find out.

During the summer of 1986 I interviewed many of the English converts in the Devon Russian Orthodox parish to discover what had led them to join so exotic a branch of Christianity. Their answers were varied. One elderly man had fallen in love with all things Russian after seeing performances of the Diaghilev ballet on tour in London in the 1920s, when Karsavina at the end of her career and Markova in her teens had astonished Covent Garden audiences. A young couple had been drawn to the Eastern faiths popular in the England of the 1960s, and after a period of meditation, vegetarianism and joss sticks were amazed to find the basic truths of the Vedanta in Orthodoxy. The disillusioned Anglicans shared the common perception of the time that the Church of England was dwindling into a secular institution for social welfare. (This was before women priests but after *Honest to God*.) What seemed to be a central core of founder members of the parish had moved from the Church of England to Roman Catholicism in search for a truth that came closer to the original; by the same process, they had then moved on to Orthodoxy, from which, as they saw it, the Western Church had broken away. The most surprising thing in the whole series of interviews was the phrase which everybody used to sum up their attitude to being part of a Russian Orthodox community: 'We feel at home here.' About ten years later I began to understand what they meant.

In the spring of 1987 we made our first visit to Patmos. This was prompted by a Christmas card we had received from

Bishop Kallistos with a brief message that he would be in the monastery there for a few weeks in early June and wondering if there was any possibility that we could meet on the island. As he was to become a central influence in my journey, I had better say a little more about him now.

As student at Oxford, Timothy Ware had taken a double first in classics and theology in spite of, he admitted to me, having fallen asleep during the final examinations. He was an Anglican at the time, but his researches into the history and teachings of the Christian Church persuaded him that the closest to the original had to be the Orthodox Church, which he joined in 1958. He wrote what has become the standard work in English, *The Orthodox Church*, published in 1963. He was ordained a priest in 1966, when he also became a monk at the Monastery of St John on Patmos.

As a schoolboy, Timothy Ware had been a frequent visitor to Felicia's home. They had become friends, and, though they had had little contact for many years, he had been the sponsor of her baptism. It was in the spirit of a family friend that he had sent his Christmas card to us with its delicately phrased invitation. I had been a fan of St John for many years, so a trip to Patmos might have special resonances for me since he had lived there in exile. We both needed a holiday, so we booked a package tour for two weeks and arrived on the island on 27 May 1987.

I should make it clear that I was not predisposed to be a pushover for the Greek scene. I had spent fifteen years living in the South Pacific, so sun-soaked islands with golden beaches fringed by azure seas held no novelty for me. I knew about getting away from it all, having been, in Fiji, as far away as it is possible to go without coming back. I found ruined temples easily resistible. In fact the whole edifice of classical Greece – the web of mythology, the Golden Age of Pericles, the Cradle of European Civilization – I found antipathetic. As a schoolboy I rejected the myths because they were untrue, and as a student I developed a strong distaste for Greek studies, based, I now realize, on the way they were put across in our educational system. To start with, they were strongly elitist. Greek was taught at our older public schools (we did Latin at Rastrick Grammar) to those who would go on to direct the activities of the Civil Service, the Conservative Party or the BBC. The alphabet was forbidding, the grammatical difficulties were horrendous; Greek, I understood, was an assault course to weed out the less able. Those who finished the course would be the natural leaders of men, destined to effortless distinction for the rest of their lives. I resented the system, having missed out on the assault course and the opportunities on offer for those who completed it.

But there was more than sour grapes in my aversion to Greek studies. I had a deep psychological antipathy to the Greeks' underlying philosophy as expressed in the motto carved over their Delphic temple, the middle-aged, middle-class, life-denying tag so beloved of desiccated classics teachers everywhere: NOTHING TO EXCESS. The classical Greeks, I believed, took great pride in their moderation, balance, proportion. They taught the measured life, lived about two degrees below normal temperature. Greek studies, I felt, were perhaps best left till the seventh age, when, sans teeth and sans natural appetites, the balanced life of quiet moderation might develop some pastel appeal.

It took no time at all on Patmos to realize that the islanders flew no flags for quiet moderation. They did tend to leave food on the restaurant tables, but this was because they ordered such mountains of it that they could not put it all away and still walk. In their zest for life they seemed unaware of age. The first Patmians we were able to talk to were all in their seventies – we could talk to them because they spoke Italian, having been at school when the island was one of Italy's overseas possessions. They would sit for hours at tables in the square sipping ouzo and occasionally getting up to dance ecstatically in a grizzled half-circle holding handkerchiefs with each other. There was something compelling about their direct way of speaking, leaning across the table

towards you, occasionally gripping your forearm to empha-
size a point, holding your eyes with theirs to be sure you
understood.

And I came to realize that expressed in all their activities
was the urgency of *now*. Life was to be lived in the present.
You could speculate about the future, though that was for
politicians. You could embroider the present with tales of the
past, and this they would do endlessly and, it seemed,
timelessly – the turning hands of the clock had no influence
on a well-spun recollection – but you were hearing it *now*.
The point of the tale was its effect on you *now*, not to
reminisce and wallow in the past. Because *now* is what
matters. *Now* is where eternity intersects with time. Not in
the past, nor in the future, but in the actively experienced
present.

One effect of this zeal for the present is that the Greeks are
loath to let it come to an end. For all of us, *now* stops when
we sleep, and I think this may be why Greeks seem to resent
going to bed. When the Greek government was debating a
law forbidding nightclubs to stay open after three a.m., in the
hope of improving productivity during the working day,
there were public demonstrations and the law had to be
abandoned. Nothing must interfere with the relishing, the
pursuit, the total commitment to the experience of *now*.

I did not realize all of this immediately, but I did feel a
strong familiarity with the zest for living so evident on
Patmos: the enthusiasm for food and drink, the joy in the
presence of a small child, the readiness to display emotion,
the eagerness to dance or sing all night. Where had I come
across this before? It was not a product of sun-soaked
islands; there was more nervous energy in it than you find
anywhere in the South Pacific. Then I remembered: the
Russians. And what was the most powerful common accul-
turating influence between the vast continental masses of
Russia and this corner of the eastern Mediterranean that
might have produced this similarity of behaviour, this

common angle of attack on life? The Orthodox church. The incarnational faith.

On Patmos, the Orthodox Church is everywhere present and influences all things. The great Monastery of St John physically dominates the island, built like a huge fortress at the summit of the central hill. But there are more integrated presences: about 400 small churches, some isolated on small offshore islands, some in village streets, some in remote hermitages and some in country districts, forming part of a complex of church and farm. Patmos has been officially declared a holy island by act of parliament, and I expected to find there a sort of brooding piety, an atmosphere of religiosity encouraged by the monastery and the Greek Tourist Board in furtherance of their different but converging aims – perhaps even an officially encouraged respect for place, such as I had found at the Kremlin.

Well, some of the tourists are different. Patmos has its share of the peeling, scarlet, backpacking youth that invade Greece every summer and enliven its streets. But there are also, on the streets here, winding columns of sombre-suited pilgrims, usually with a priest in attendance, who visit the Cave of the Apocalypse and the Monastery of St John as part of their spiritual tour. As for the Patmians, the natives of the island, they have integrated their faith into their daily lives for centuries, until there is no such thing as a secular activity. If you ask them how they are, they will tend to reply 'Well,' and add the words '*Dhoxa to Theo*' – 'Glory to God'. And if you make any plans for the future, even to see somebody the next day, they will add '*An theli o Theos*' – 'God willing'. There was certainly nothing remotely pietistic about Patmian behaviour, no sense of that reserve, of remoteness from the everyday, we often associate with practising, especially professional, Christians in England: a slight feeling that, no matter how intense or appealing any secular experience might be – a gulp of draught beer, a Dorset landscape, a really good joke – there is a Greater Reality which alone deserves our total commitment. Patmians, I fancy, find the Greater Reality in the beer, the landscape and the joke.

Perhaps I might digress with an anecdote here to justify what I say about the other-worldliness of professional Christians in England. I went to England on leave from Fiji in the 1960s and visited my brother Bill, who lives in the West Riding of Yorkshire. He took me for a drink to his cricket club, and shortly after we arrived he left me standing at the bar. I turned to strike up a conversation with a small group of men standing next to me. Although they were pleasant enough, I thought I detected a reserve, an artificiality, a slight tension in the way they spoke to me. I moved over to another, slightly noisier, group who were swapping stories. It was lunchtime and the draught beer was going down well. As I stood listening, the belly laughs changed to chuckles and then to smiles and nods. They spoke to me in a friendly way, and yet there was something inhibited and unnatural about the way they spoke and their body language when I was close by. Now our Bill has a reputation in the family for practical jokes, and I went to him for an explanation. 'What did you tell them about me?' 'Oh,' he said, 'I had to explain the posh voice, so I just told them you were a parson!' Bill's little joke gave me direct experience of the way the professionally religious are treated in our society. If, as social psychologists tell us, our characters are formed by the expectations and reactions of others, then it is little wonder our parsons tend to be other-worldly.

But back to Patmos. The impressions I have been remembering made their impact in our first two weeks on the island. I sometimes think that you can get the feel of a strange country accurately in a very short time on a first visit. You become quickly aware of the essentials when they are unfamiliar and uncluttered with detail. It can take ten years' residence to learn anything that adds significantly to those first impressions. We had seen enough to be quite sure that Patmos had a part to play in our lives. We booked another package tour in the autumn of 1987, and during the ten days we spent on the island we bought a small house in the village of Chora, which surrounds the monastery. I had a commission to write a book which would keep me busy during the summer months on the island, and I hoped to find enough work in broadcasting during the winters in England.

The first priority was to learn Greek. During the English winter I launched myself confidently enough on a language course of books and cassettes. I had found French easy as a schoolboy, and had managed a fair working knowledge of Fijian in a couple of years. I thought Greek might take me three or four. I was wrong. Either those bits of the brain that handle new languages atrophy with increasing age and consumption of alcohol or fresh vegetables, or Greek is particularly inaccessible, or both. In my very first steps in Greek I stumbled against so many perversities: how, for example, in any European language, could the word *nai* possibly mean 'yes', and a raising of the eyebrows with a slight nod of the head mean 'no'? I found the syntax incomprehensible and the vast array of irregular verbs daunting. Some people, I gather, learn languages by first mastering their essential structure and then building a vocabulary. It is for such people that grammar books are written. I have never been able to understand these books, and my own approach to a new language has to be by simple imitation. I listen to other people and try to remember what they say – just like small children do. The method works well enough when you are surrounded by people speaking the language you want to learn and your brain is young, fresh and retentive. At my age, listening to a cassette in a car while driving along a Devon lane, progress was laggard.

Then I remembered my experience with the Latin New Testament on the *Southern Cross*. Perhaps it would help to read, in Greek, words I already knew in English. So I began reading a Greek New Testament with a literal translation into English printed underneath the Greek words. This did not produce any linguistic advances of use in the local supermarket, but it did give me some startling insights into the real meaning of texts I thought I understood.

The most exciting was Matthew 16:19, where Christ says to Peter, 'I will give you the keys of the kingdom of heaven, and whatever you bind on earth shall be bound in heaven, and whatever you loose on earth shall be loosed in heaven.' These words are at the foundation of the claims to papal authority. And, even though the same power of binding and loosing was promised to the other Apostles (Matthew 18:18), Peter alone received the keys of the kingdom and the promise that his personal dictates in moral and spiritual matters would be subsequently authorized by divine authority. It is an awesome text. It seems to justify the breathtaking claim that one man's personal decisions will receive celestial endorsement. But the claim is based on a loose translation. In the Greek text, Jesus tells Peter that 'what he binds on earth' will be 'what has been bound in heaven'. In other words, the promise is not that Peter's binding and loosing will be observed by heaven so that they can be subsequently ratified there, but – a very different statement – that Peter's decisions would be in accordance with the divine dispensation: that they would be right.

Reading St John's Gospel in Greek was exciting in a way I had not expected. Of course the intense spirituality came over more richly as I began to understand the resonances of the Greek words. But I had accepted that the fourth Gospel was the last to be written, the most spiritually advanced, the most carefully crafted, least spontaneous of the accounts of events in the life of Jesus because it was the furthest removed from the events it describes. When working through the Greek version I began to notice telling irrelevances which seemed inappropriate to a carefully crafted script. Why, in the record of the raising of Lazarus, does John hold up the story by bothering to mention that, as Jesus approached Bethany, Martha went out to meet him while Mary stayed in the house? Why, when the Samaritan woman goes off to the city to tell the people that Jesus knows all she ever did, does John mention that she left her water jug behind? Why, in the moment of high drama, when Jesus is taken to the court of the high priest, does he put in the little scene with the servants warming themselves at a charcoal fire which they had made because it was cold? Why, at the climax of the resurrection story, the discovery of the empty tomb, does he bother to mention that John ran faster than Peter to get to the tomb but waited outside when he got there and that only when Peter entered the tomb did he notice that the napkin which had covered Jesus's face was not with the linen cloths but lying rolled up in a separate place? These details do not sit easily in a Gospel which has been described as a pervadingly allegorical and mystical meditation on the teaching of Christ. They are rather the small irrelevances that hang about in the memory of somebody who was there.

The stories may not on that account be true: there could be lapses of memory in an eyewitness, or even invention of incidents likely to further the propaganda message. But there would be no point in inventing details which add nothing to the propaganda and hold up the pace of the story. I could have noticed these things in an English translation, of course, but it was only when working carefully through the Greek that they made their impact. I could no longer accept the Gospel of St John as a mystical meditation, a skilful allegory written a century after the death of Christ to promote a particular version of the Christian story. Whoever wrote it, I decided, was there, as he claimed, when these things happened.

Churches are well attended on Patmos, but mostly by women and children. Equality of participation by the sexes tends to happen only on major feast days. There is quite a lot of moving about and some casual chattering in the services. A feast day is a social as well as a religious occasion, or perhaps there is no distinction made. We attended the Sunday-morning liturgies and any feast days in our locality. Felicia would participate in the service and I would try to follow them in a Greek/English version. There were many external beauties – the dark glowing icons, the heady incense, the many candles and the rich robes of the priest – but it took a long time for the charms of Byzantine chanting to become evident. After the sweet harmonies of Russian church music, the singing on Patmos seemed harsh, tonally insecure and always too loud. But there was this same combination of a matter-of-factness about the ceremonies and a high seriousness of purpose that I found fascinating. I suppose it was a product of centuries of doing the same thing which had made the doing of it totally familiar – members of the congregation would sometimes shout the next words of a Gospel passage as it was being read – coupled with the acceptance that what they were doing was participating in a miracle, getting in touch with the eternal. Experiencing God.

The culture of Patmos is steeped in Orthodoxy. This has produced extremists who seem aroused by Orthodox practices more than they would be by those of, say, the Church of England. And so, while we have examples on the island of the gentle kindliness of Starets Zossima, we also occasionally come across the wild-eyed fanaticism of Father Ferrapont. Sometimes, at Easter, converts from Western Christianity will appear, haggard from excessive fasting. And then there are those who see the Common Market as an indication that the destruction of the world is at hand and point to the bar code as a cypher for the number 666, the Sign of the Beast. Such ideas are imported, but they tend to find a ready, though small, audience on the island.

More generally, it seemed to me that the influence of Orthodoxy had been towards a clear-sighted, unjudgemental view of people. On a small island, characters are easy to assess, actions stay in the collective memory, reputations are painted in strong colours. So an honest man will be described as such: *Eine sostos!*, with a gesture making a circle of thumb and forefinger and drawing in the air a strong straight vertical line. A tricky one is *poniros*, the right hand extended, weaving away from the body like a snake. But admiration for the honest man is often tinged with reserve, a hint that he could have done better for himself and his family if he had a touch more guile. And the *poniros* is never condemned, only given the label so that we can be on our guard. I came to realize that these attitudes spring from what seems like a flexible approach to morality in the Orthodox Church. That is to say not that its concepts of right and wrong are fuzzy, but that it doesn't expect people to behave always with moral correctness. When they stray, the duty of the Church is not to condemn them but to get them back again on the right path. There is even within Orthodox canon law a practice called 'economy', which signifies a departure from the rules of the Church in order to assist the salvation of a particular person.

All this seems very strange and rather suspect to someone with a background in Western Christianity. I personally found it scandalous when I first came across it. After all, the solace of my early repressed years in the straitjacket of Methodism had been the reassurance that the rich would have a hard time of it in the next life. God had promised this, and God was just. And one of the attractions of Roman Catholicism to me had been the strict legality with which the commandments of a just God were dispensed. My volumes on moral theology allotted precise penalties for a vast range of human sins. I took great comfort from the assiduity with which the recording angel kept tag and a just God dispensed penalties. My pitifully acute sense of justice, which I have mentioned, relished the fine old words 'Vengeance is mine; I will repay, saith the Lord.' Whatever wrongs escaped retribution in this life would be sure to be paid for in the next. Christians, I thought, tended to root their ethics in divine commandments. The ten which God gave to Moses when he descended on Mount Sinai in fire and smoke to the sound of trumpets were still repeated in the Christian catechism. God, according to the Christians I had met and studied, is the Supreme Judge who rewards the good and punishes the wicked. Salvation comes from sticking to the rules.

When I discovered that the Orthodox Church places a

different emphasis on ethical behaviour, and one which takes account of individual situations, I thought at first that it was simply bowing to the fashion of the time, when what were called 'situation ethics' were popular and rules were being relaxed all round. But the Orthodox church could never, I quickly realized, be accused of being trendy. And the concept of 'economy' which so much disturbed me went back at least 1,500 years.

As I learned more about it, I discovered the Orthodox teaching that rules of conduct, for the Christian, have a secondary character. When we are told that we should become perfect even as our Heavenly Father is perfect, this does not mean simply that we stick to the rules – perfection refers to an inner spiritual condition, not to outward conduct (though, of course, the inner changes are reflected in outward actions). The attainment of perfection (which, in the Greek means not 'faultlessness' but 'completion') of the inner life is a common task, but we each have our individual personality to bring to completion. Two people may appear do the same thing but it is not the same thing, because it has to be seen in relation to the inner spiritual condition of each. So the commandment not to judge is not merely a moral injunction, it is based on the fact that we cannot know that which is the subject of judgement: the inner and individually unique spiritual condition.

Of course, moral values as the directing principles of human life are extremely important, but in the practice and teaching of the Orthodox Church the living person is more important than the principles of moral conduct. Judgement is there, but it is not the pronouncement of a transcendental tribunal or a just God determining a person's fate from the outside: it is the immanent consequence of the choice made by an individual. The person who has rejected belief is condemned already, and the condemnation is self-inflicted because he has cut himself off from the light. The gates of hell, as has been noted, are locked on the *inside*.

This unfamiliar attitude to morality explains the Orthodox

love for the Prodigal Son. I think, if we are honest, the story is an uncomfortable one for many of us in the West. We feel, don't we, that the elder brother gets a raw deal. He, after all, has faithfully served his father for many years, slaving in the fields without reward, whereas the young one who has taken his share of the family fortune and squandered it comes home to music and dancing and the fatted calf. It is an unjust tale. But the point of it is that God's relation to man is not of judgement but of love. Sin is a disease or a danger from which the repentant sinner has recovered. Love is given not in response to the merit but to the need of the person. So the Prodigal Son is given more because he needs more. This is unjust. But God is love.

Even worse is the story about the labourers in the vineyard. How can we, with our sense of justice, accept that workers who turn up late in the afternoon should get the same daily wages as the ones who started first thing in the morning? The Orthodox attitude is expressed in the sermon by St John Chrysostom read every year at the Easter service:

> Whoever is a devout lover of God, let him enjoy this beautiful bright festival . . . If any have toiled from the first hour, let him receive his due reward. If any have come after the third hour, let him with gratitude join the feast. And he that arrived after the sixth hour, let him not doubt, for he shall sustain no loss. And if any have delayed until the ninth hour, let him not hesitate but let him come too. And he that hath arrived only at the eleventh hour, let him not be afraid by reason of his delay; for the Lord is gracious and receiveth the last as the first.

It just isn't fair. This may be Christianity, but it is not justice. But of course it is Christianity. And it is unjust. Thank God. As Hamlet says, 'Use every man after his deserts, and who should 'scape whipping?' We can none of us deserve salvation, we can none of us earn it. We can only hope for it as an undeserved gift, like the party for the Prodigal Son.

All of these aspects of Orthodox teaching slowly became

clear to me on Patmos, through reading books and discussions with local priests and people. They appealed to me. I felt increasingly drawn to them. But I was still approaching Christianity as an observer, sympathetic, increasingly aware of the subtleties of what was going on, keen to learn, but unconvinced of the existence of those supernatural forces which those around me perceived as realities. I suppose it was not all that different from my anthropological studies in Fiji, with the important difference that my wife subscribed to beliefs which I found unpersuasive. Neither she nor I would have wanted me to change on that account.

Then I met Father Amphilochios Tsoukos. He was a monk priest at the Monastery of St John who taught at the theological school. He had the unusual habit of secretly distributing his salary to the poor, because he had no need of it and because, as a monk, he was committed to a life of poverty. He would occasionally accept small gifts to please the donors, and the Patmians would sometimes, as a sort of game, give him a propelling pencil or a ballpoint pen, to see how many hours it would be before he passed it on. He spoke a little French, having worked as a missionary in the French territories of Africa, and so when we first met at a very basic level we were able to communicate. What immediately impressed me about him was a great sense of delight he took in all things – flowers, children, every person he spoke to. And those who met him felt that delight and were warmed by it, including me.

He quickly decided, after our first meeting, that I must teach him English and he would teach me Greek. I should go to his cell at the monastery twice a week in the afternoons for the lessons. When I arrived, he would insist that we have coffee before starting the lesson. This coffee took a long time to prepare as his kitchen facilities were rudimentary. Then he would suggest a small sweetmeat or half a cucumber before getting down to work, and then he would tell me of things that had happened to him that day and ask how we were settling in at the house. By the time we had got through the coffee, the cucumber and the gossip, the hour set apart for the lesson would be past and he would suggest we really get down to things next time. After a few weeks I realized that he did not really want to learn English. The 'lessons' were an excuse to bring us together for a brief time twice a week. He felt that this was important, and that something would result from it. By making me coffee and chatting about trivia he was disconnecting my analytical brain from what was going on, just as Tim Galway had distracted my mind on the tennis court in Hollywood. He thought that if we just spent time together I might absorb something. He was right.

Quite soon after we met, I interviewed him 'in depth' as I would have approached a contributor to the *Everyman* series. He was a promising interviewee: an unusually committed person, firmly rooted in a Christian faith which shaped his every waking hour, with what seemed to be a medieval austerity about him, and yet bubbling with life and completely lacking in censoriousness or self-righteousness. He had worked as missionary among primitive tribes in Africa, so it seemed fair to talk to him about his techniques for passing on the Christian message to unbelievers. As an unbeliever myself, I faced him with what seemed to me to be an unsolvable but highly relevant problem for the Christian missionary today.

Through an interpreter, I explained that I was a member of a vast modern tribe which had an unprecedented awareness of the human psyche. We had discovered and analysed the workings of the mind, conscious and unconscious, so that we knew that religious faith was no more than a compensatory mechanism giving reassurance to the insecure. We could not be deceived by myths, however powerful their archetypal resonances. We sought the truth, and saw no virtue in putting our trust in that for which there was insufficient evidence. Christianity was not strange to us – our society had been fundamentally Christian for 1,500 years – but we had carefully examined and, after careful research, rejected the basic principles of the faith of our ancestors. And we had done so in the fearless pursuit of truth. If you came as a missionary to my tribe, I asked, what would be your approach or line of argument? 'I would not argue with you,' he said simply, 'I would just be with you. And I would love you.'

Now, at any time during the previous forty years of my inquiries into religious truth I should have dismissed this answer as evasive. Had I still been working in the context of my role as as reporter on *Everyman*, I should have reacted with a tolerant smile and followed up with a few subsidiary questions to make it clear that I was dealing with an 'ineffable', who could not contribute to a dispassionate and rational inquiry, before moving on to more televisual material. But when I heard those words, from that man, at that time, I experienced a shift in understanding rather like the impact of great music. I suddenly understood the Christian claim that God is love; and we cannot know God with our minds but we might experience his energies through love. I remembered the words in *The Cloud of Unknowing*. 'By love may he be gotten and holden, but by thought, never.'

Here we come to one of those crucial moments of personal experience which are difficult to put into words and which, I suppose, could be characterized as authoritative for me and irrelevant to anybody else. It is at this point that I have so consistently felt the keenest disappointment in reading the spiritual journeys of others. When Wesley felt his heart 'strangely warmed' or C. S. Lewis came down from the upper deck of that bus in Headington with his faith firmly in place I just felt, as a reader, left behind. At the key moment when I needed to understand exactly why a change had happened, a basic reorientation of personality had been brought about, there was no explanation. Or at least not one which I found accessible. But any reader who has stayed with me this long deserves better. So let me try to make what happened comprehensible by examining what exactly the shift of understanding was.

I had first read those words from *The Cloud of Unknowing* at Oxford, thirty-five years before I spoke to Father Amphilochios. I had copied them into a commonplace book. I had read many times since then the identification of God with love, especially in St John, whose Gospel I admired so much. But the words meant nothing to me, because, I suppose, I was not ready for them. We must all read and hear in the course of our lives enough truths to give us wisdom, but they can have no effect on us if we are not receptive. We may think we have open minds, that a reasoned logical argument will lead us to a correct interpretation of reality, but we select the tools of our understanding out of our own tool kit. We may make a bad selection or be inadequately equipped. So we read or hear the words and pass on in ignorance. Another passage from my commonplace book is by William Temple:

A high ideal may be presented to a man and he considers whether or not he shall accept it for the guidance of his life. His answer must depend upon his character. He may give the truest and wisest answer of which he is capable; but if he has allowed himself to settle down to a selfish outlook or to materialist standards, this will affect his judgement. He will reject the ideal in perfect sincerity; but that sincerity is not so much a justification of his conduct but a measure of his sin.

When Father Amphilochios spoke of love as a way to bring people into contact with faith, I understood what he meant because I was at last equipped to do so. I realized that this was not a woolly 'ineffable' way of dodging the question of how to approach religious truth but a perfectly sane and rational response. The most basic principle of learning is that we start with the known and move to the unknown. To begin an inquiry into the truth of Christianity, as I had done, by examining the arguments for the existence of God, which seemed the logical first step and was the approach of the scholastics, was to tackle the question from the wrong end. It was starting with the unknown, possibly the unknowable. No wonder I had made so little progress in forty years. Father

Amphilochios proposed that the journey to Christian truth should start with the human experience of love: to move, that is, from the known to the unknown.

By the time he spoke to me that day on Patmos, I had learned and forgotten many things; I was attracted by but could not accept the claims of the Church he represented; I had no faith in any supernatural entities; I rejected all certainties with the old tag from Bertrand Russell: 'If you're certain about anything you're certainly wrong, because nothing deserves certainty . . .' But wait. There was one certainty in my life. One reality which did not need to be authenticated by rational or philosophical argument because I knew it had to be true from experience. And it was the most important reality in my life: my love for Felicia. This could not be expressed in words or explained by biochemistry or depth psychology. I could never make anyone else, perhaps not even her, completely understand the nature of that reality. I knew it from experience. I knew that for over twenty years it had enriched and brightened the whole of my life and called for the best in me. If I attempted to analyse or understand it myself, using my rational intelligence, I failed. And yet the certainty endured. I was aware of it every day. But I could grasp its reality at the centre of my being only by using all my faculties together – the 'integral cognition' of Kireyeksy; the 'heart, mind and soul' of less technical speech. So I had to accept that there are truths which we can directly experience and accept on the authority of that experience. Love is one of them, and that points, perhaps, to others.

The immediate objection to the notion of love as a reality is that it is no more than a word which describes a purely subjective state. I can know that I am in love exactly as I know that I have a headache. Neither the love nor the headache exists outside myself, therefore I cannot claim that either has an objective reality apart from myself. I had long accepted that religious faith is a similar subjective condition which attaches itself to imagined entities without objective existence.

But the basic assumption behind this scepticism is one which, although very common, is wrong. It accepts that every reality must be part either of an outer, objective, material world or of an inner, mental one. This seems to be self-evident. But there are telling exceptions. The feelings which I experienced when hearing the prelude to *The Mastersingers* or seeing the *Virgin of the Rocks* were, of course, subjective. But they were distinct from the aesthetic reality which Wagner and Leonardo sought to convey. This, the content of a work of art, that which a composer seeks to embody in his music and performers try to interpret, is neither a mood nor an emotion nor a material thing in the external world. Yet it is undeniably a reality. And one that endures.

So my scepticism, which insisted on an answer to the question of whether the reality of the content of religious experience is 'objective' or 'subjective', turned out to be based on too narrow a view of reality. If by 'objective' we mean that which exists in the external world and can be verified by the senses coupled with scientific instruments, if by 'subjective' we mean that which forms part of our mental life and is dependent on us, then the content of religious experience, like the content of aesthetic or moral experience, is neither objective nor subjective. And yet these experiences, realities, affect our lives more profoundly than anything else. Not everyone is equally sensitive to them, but that does not, of course, affect their existence. A person may be tone-deaf, but that does not diminish the reality of the power and beauty of a Mozart adagio.

So, after talking with Father Amphilochios, I had reached the stage of accepting the existence of realities which my rational mind could not comprehend. Further, I came to recognize something I had forgotten since childhood: that the most exciting, profoundly moving, ultimately important influences in my life were the ones I could not completely understand. They alone deserved wonder, and wonder was not to be dismissed as juvenile but to be embraced as the only appropriate mature adult response to life.

I think it was at about this time that I came to realize that, although I could not accept the claims of Christianity, although I had reasoned myself out of any truck with the supernatural, most of the people I had felt close to in my past or were attracted to in the present had what I would have called a 'spiritual dimension' to their character. Which was strange. I remembered that C. S. Lewis had written that he was puzzled to find, as an unbeliever, that the people he most enjoyed were Christians: Coghill and Chesterton. Beside them he found Shaw and Wells, Gibbon and Voltaire a little thin – what he and his schoolboy friends called 'tinny'. I found from my own experience that the believers I knew had a warmth in their characters, a life in their eyes, a paradoxical combination of understanding and wonderment that I was beginning to admire. They may be deluded, I thought, but they get a great deal out of life. And just how certain could I be that they were deluded?

I had reached the stage of turning my natural scepticism on to scepticism itself. The self-assurance of the intellectual debunkers of Christianity was no longer convincing. I found reductionist scientific materialism simple-minded and naive. To reject all knowledge which did not come to us through the intellect was unintelligent. Certainties, I realized, were possible if they were directly experienced. On the other hand, I was repelled by what struck me as superstition and credulity. If it was wrong to rely solely on the intellect in a search for truth, then it was just as wrong to leave intelligence behind. I could not place my trust or even hope in the intellectually absurd. I needed a licence to believe.

Chapter Eight

God was always the problem. I had spent over forty years trying to work out if he existed, not as an urgent quest with top priority but simply as one of the more interesting unanswered questions life threw up. I seemed to be having a full and enjoyable time without him. I had, so far as I was aware, no unfulfilled emotional or spiritual needs. I was not concerned about the afterlife, since it seemed to me overwhelmingly probable that death was simply a sleep from which you didn't wake up. But I was still intrigued by the vast number of people, past and present, who claimed, so far as I could tell in all honesty, to have found him. In my experience, religious people had in common a basic belief in God and then were, for the most part, culturally divided as to whether they went on to claim that Krishna was his avatar, Muhammad was his prophet or Christ was his son. I had studied and sympathized with them all. But I couldn't even take the first step.

Faith in God, according to my theological books, was a gift from God. I had not yet received it. The Roman Catholic Church had at first raised my hopes by telling me that God could be found by the unaided use of the human reason, but had then disappointed me by not coming up with sufficient proofs of his existence. Father Michael, of the Russian Orthodox Church, had written out for me a little prayer and asked if I would say it with him. It began, 'O Heavenly King, the Comforter, the Spirit of Truth . . .' But, for all my affection for Father Michael, I couldn't say it, because I felt dishonest and a little foolish addressing a being who did not exist. I did try for a time the unbeliever's plaintive request: 'God, if you exist, please let me know.' But couldn't keep it up, for the same reason. I had finally come to the point of accepting the existence of entities not accessible to the rational mind, but it had taken me forty years to get there. I had arrived only through putting a serious workload on my rational processes in trying to keep up with the Russian epistemologists, and I was not ready immediately to rush out and find fairies at the bottom of my garden.

There is a story told at Oxford of the head of one of the colleges there greeting a new intake of students. He told them that if they were diligent and applied themselves to their studies they would, on leaving the university, acquire a degree. He went on, 'and you will then know when a man is talking rot. To be able to tell when a man is talking rot is, to many people, the main, and to me the sole, purpose of an education.' In the playful aphorism of a waggish don there is a significant truth: the main function of the intellect is to discriminate. Perhaps the reason will not lead us into all truth, but it may protect us from error. In my case, my intellectual approach had not led me to accept the existence of God, but at least it had prevented me from finding him where he wasn't.

Truth had always seemed to me all-important. This was not a noble philosophical ideal but a visceral instinct going back as far as I can remember. Possibly it was rooted in or inspired by my father's passion for truth which had led him to ban baby talk and fairy tales. It was a pursuit of truth which had led me to admire Bertrand Russell, to join the British Humanist Association, to plough through books on epistemology which I could only half understand.

Having failed to establish the existence of God by philosophical argument, I was left with the 'leap of faith'. Religious people have often pointed out to me that belief is necessary where rational certainty is impossible. And they go on to suggest that it is spiritually admirable to put your trust in that which cannot be proved, which may therefore be doubted, and often is. But I always found something unwholesome about the notion that faith is meritorious because it means accepting that for which there is no sound evidence. The most celebrated example of this attitude is Tertullian, with his famous dictum *Certum est quia impossible est* – 'It is certain because it is impossible.' But Tertullian was fond of paradoxes and eventually argued himself into heresy. His approach to truth leads to the achievement of the White Queen, who, with practice, could believe as many as six impossible things before breakfast.

In the summer of 1988, on Patmos, I was reviewing all these ideas, the accumulation of forty years of reading, thinking and talking about religion. Although I could not take the first step and believe in God, I had come to an awareness of the uniqueness of Christ and of the Christian message. After going off on the long-winded and fatuous pursuit of the 'historical Jesus' in the company of earnest nineteenth-century German professors and failing to find him, I had passed through a period of trying to demythologize him and distil his essential message as proclaimed by the school of Rudolf Bultmann. Finally, I had stopped reading the critics and gone back to St John, to meet a powerful, consistent, living personality of unmatched simplicity and profundity.

I had accepted by then that, so far as I could judge them, the effects of Orthodox Christianity on the people I knew were positive. Their lives were enhanced and not diminished by it. The teaching and practice of the Orthodox Church seemed to me to embody the original Christian revelation. And I had direct experience of the truth of insights which came from the Orthodox perspective. One of the most telling was from Bishop Kallistos, who told me that the things we treasure most in our lives are not the ones we have earned but the ones we have been given. In my own life, the most precious, constantly exciting, fundamentally secure reality is my love for Felicia – which I did not intend, plan or design. I can claim no credit for it. It can fairly be called a free gift. The same goes for the friendships I've been lucky enough to experience, and the music and the paintings and the food and the sunsets. These are all unearned: the gifts.

In the summer of 1988 I was aware of the gifts but not of the Giver. And it was becoming obvious to me – it had been obvious to everyone else for years – that if I wanted to understand more, to be receptive to the spiritual influences of the Orthodox Church, then I should stop peering through the window and step inside.

One morning, just as the sun was burning off the mists that creep up the mountain, I looked out and saw the familiar truck loaded with vegetables slowly climbing the road towards the village. From a battered old metal loudspeaker on the roof a crackling distorted voice was shouting, '*Elate na theete*', 'Come and see.' And I thought how direct and striking this invitation was in an age of sophisticated advertising. There was no hard sell involved, no exaggerated claims that what was on the truck would make you glamorous, rich or wrinkle-free. Simply a statement – 'I have apples, pears, bananas, cabbages' – and an invitation: 'Come and see.' Come and check out the goods for yourself. When you have seen, you can decide for yourself whether or not to buy. Here is what is on offer. Make up your own mind. Just come and see for yourself.

The words rang a faint bell in my memory, and then I remembered. They were the words Jesus first spoke to the two disciples of John who inquired about him. The same words as Philip spoke to Nathaniel when he asked about Jesus. 'Come and see.' Perhaps this was the invitation I should take up. Stop reading about Christianity, don't consult any more theologians or philosophers, don't sit outside the Church reading the Bible and trying to puzzle out through philological studies what it has to say. Come in. Come and see.

The Church, I had been told by theologians, was a channel

of grace. If I joined it, that grace would become available to me. Through it, I might at last come to believe in God. But the problem was that I had to declare my belief in him before I was allowed in. So I was faced, in the summer of 1988, with a neat circular problem: to progress further I should join the Church; entrance to the Church was through baptism; after baptism I should receive the grace to believe in God. But I had to declare my belief in God by reciting the Creed *before* baptism. This I could not, in honesty, do. The problem seemed to me not only neat but insoluble.

I put it to Bishop Kallistos in a letter from Patmos. He replied by return. He thought that I had spent enough time studying Orthodoxy from the outside. He knew of the progress I had made and the difficulties I was facing. My *kairos*, he wrote, had come. (The word means an appropriate time in one's life to do something. It is the word used in Ecclesiastes in the passage 'a time to be born, and a time to die; a time to plant and a time to pluck up that which is planted'). He would baptize me, if I wished, on his visit to Patmos in September. As for the Creed, there was a perfectly simple solution: if I could not recite it for myself then he, if I would trust him, would do it for me. I should come to understand it later.

I was, of course, shocked by the suggestion. The Creed had always been a barrier for me since those years in the choir at St John's Church, Clifton, when I crossed my fingers in order to recite it. The truth was all-important. I knew that I could not at my baptism solemnly profess a belief I did not have, and it seemed dishonest to have somebody else do it for me. I felt a certain pride in my integrity on this question.

But Bishop Kallistos was not a man to propose anything dishonest. He was a man of great learning, and through his role as a confessor he had wide experience of people's spiritual conditions. It was possible, even likely, that he knew more about my own spiritual state than I did myself, because I had kept constantly in touch with him and he had more discernment and experience than I. Besides, I could hardly turn round to a distinguished scholar, theologian, priest and bishop of the Orthodox Church and suggest that I knew more than he did about the conditions of entry. I agreed to put my trust in him and to be baptized.

The tradition of the Orthodox Church is that adults are baptized in their shrouds, so that the garment in which you receive new life is that in which your body will be buried. This gave us a problem, because none of the Patmos drapers seemed to have shrouds in stock and when we asked if they could make up one in my size they all reacted with alarm about my health. In the end, Felicia bought a single sheet and sewed up a shroud out of it. My Orthodox friends here wanted me to be baptized in the sea at the roadside site where St John is said to have baptized, but I was too timid to create a scene in public and we settled for the small chapel of St Irene in Scala, which was in the care of a particular friend, Sister Agathangeli. As there is no font in the church, someone brought along a forty-four-gallon oil drum and filled it with lukewarm water.

The service began at seven a.m. Father Amphilochios was there as well as Bishop Kallistos and three other priests who had become friends. Sister Agathangeli supervised the arrangements and the solicitous ladies who from time to time dipped their elbows into the drum and went tut-tutting up to the house for another kettle of hot water. I had a grey mist in front of my eyes before the service, like the one that accompanies a migraine. When I plunged into the water it dissipated. The ladies told me it was the devil at work; I thought it just possibly caused by tension and having got out of bed at 5.30 am.

There was no blinding revelation at my baptism. I was affected by the emotion of sheer pleasure that I caught from the faces of the friends there – to be the cause of delight is itself delightful – I was not conscious of grace descending as a warm glow or a cool breeze. But I felt somehow equipped to carry on the search, perhaps more receptive to whatever wisdom or insights the practice of Christianity from within might bring.

The insights came quickly. Possibly they came from an infusion of grace through the reception of the sacraments and the operation of the Holy Spirit, or possibly – because any miraculous explanation must have a rational alternative if we are to keep our free will – I simply began to find plausible those views of reality which had local social support: what sociologists call 'that vexed connection between what we believe and who we sup with'. I shall try to put these insights into words. They will not convince the steadfast unbeliever, because free will demands the capacity to deny, but I would ask the reader who has stayed with me this far to simply engage with them. It is, as I discovered, through engagement with the experience of others that we find our own way.

The first and all-important insight that came along concerned the nature of Christian truth. I was grateful for it, because it was precisely an attachment to truth that had kept me outside the Church for so long. It had always seemed to me that, however attractive, however morally correct, the teachings of the Christian Church might be, they had to be rejected because they were based on an illusion: the existence of God. There were hints in books by Christians that their understanding of 'truth' was somehow different from the secular one, and I had always assumed that this was simply an instance of moving the goalposts: to put it simply, Christians had a peculiar notion of truth which allowed them to accept that for which there was no good evidence.

But when Christ said, 'I am the way, the truth, and the life' what did he mean? Clearly his notion of truth was not ours. When he said to Pilate, 'Every one who is of the truth hears my voice,' Pilate was understandably puzzled as to what he meant. For Pilate, truth was simply a statement which accorded with reality. He reacted to Christ's claim with the question 'What is truth?' This was not a jest but a perfectly reasonable request for additional information, because the word was being used in a way unfamiliar to him. 'Truth', for Christ, had a special meaning.

The word which became flesh and dwelt among us is described as 'full of grace and truth'; Moses, we are told, brought the Law, but 'grace and truth came through Jesus Christ'. The Greek word used is *alithea*. It clearly means something more profound than the simple correspondence of words with facts. I had to discover what Christ meant by it.

As usual, I turned to books, and found that the early usage of the word *alithea* in the poetry of Homer, tended to oppose it to a lie; but later writers, including Antiphon, Thucydides and Plato, use it in a more significant way: to mean reality as opposed to appearance. This takes us back to the oldest religious insight in the world, that of the Vedanta, which I had come across in Fiji forty years before. The world perceived by our senses is only a small part of total reality. There exists an eternal or ideal world beyond it, and those who are deceived into thinking that the world of the senses, the world of appearance, is the only reality are victims of what the Hindus call *maya*, or illusion. The world which we perceive with our senses is limited by our organs of perception.

This ancient religious insight has the support of twentieth-century science. From Sir Russell's Brain's book *Mind, Perception and Science*, I had noted:

Our knowledge of the external world is based on perceptions which depend on the physical structure of the sense organs and nervous system. This in itself constitutes a limit to our perceptions; and it is likely enough that it sets bounds to our thought also. Need we believe that a nervous system evolved to facilitate action upon the physical world is capable of providing conceptual symbols adequate for the whole of reality? He is a bold man who would claim that today.

We have an incomplete awareness of reality because of the limitations of our perceptual apparatus and the limitations of our conceptions of space, time and causality. Our perceptions are subjective and partial. But we can think of them as such only if there exists an objective and complete reality which exists beyond our ability to perceive it. This insight is shared by Taoism, Hinduism and Christianity. It is either a curiously widespread and tenacious delusion into which independent cultures in different parts of the world have inexplicably and it seems inextricably tumbled or it is a genuine insight perceived by these cultures and shared by the greatest of Western philosophers, including Plato, Kant and Schopenhauer. It is this view of reality, I suddenly realized, which Christ means by the truth.

Christian truth, then, is not a concordance of words with facts but of the mind with reality: to be in the truth is to see things as they really are. This is the truth that sets people free. The freedom is from error, from *maya*. The most exciting truth I have discovered is contained in St John's Gospel, which I have loved for forty years thinking it to be mystical poetry but now can embrace as true. It speaks of, and puts the reader, the listener, in contact with truth.

Quite soon after I came to understand the meaning of truth as the ultimate reality, beyond our limited perceptions, I remembered that Gandhi used to say, 'Truth is God.' I did not understand the words when I first read them, but Gandhi's views on spiritual matters deserved respect and I had remembered them. They suddenly were full of significance, because if I had come to an understanding of truth, and if Gandhi was right, I had at the same time, and without realizing it, accepted the reality of God.

This acceptance was based, like all our knowledge, on authority and experience. Most of what we know we take on trust from books or from people. This knowledge is subject to change and amendment as we acquire more information. The authority on which it is based comes from our assessment of the credibility of the sources. It seems to me that the sources which assert the existence of a reality beyond our senses, having made this assertion from widely different perspectives and maintained it over a time span as long as the history of civilization, possess a high degree of credibility.

The experience that underpinned my acceptance was that of direct contact with beauty and with goodness. Such contact has an effect completely different in kind and intensity from sensual pleasure. Great music produces in me the sensation of being in immediate contact with a reality which is transcendental, not expressible in words. I had the same experience when coming into the presence of great sculpture: the statue of Hermes at Olympia. The encounter with goodness has the same effect. I have been lucky enough to meet people with serene commitment to goodness, and they inspire in me the same feelings as great music or sculpture. The feelings are called by philosophers 'the immanent experience of a transcendental reality'. For me, the inescapable fact is that they are realities. I know that beauty and goodness exist because I experience them, as I experience joy and pain. They are supersensory realities which present themselves directly to me. I do not think, surmise or believe in their existence: I know them directly. This knowledge is not subject to amendment.

Because these experiences have a transcendental quality, it is not unreasonable to accept, as the wisest men of the past have suggested, that they are promptings from the ultimate reality, breaks in the clouds which allow us a brief experience of that which is eternal and ineffable. The Orthodox would say they are the energies of God. I now find that I experience them every day.

When I hold in the palm of my hand what my brain and a botanical dictionary tell me is a short-stalked white flower with a green calyx with awl-shaped teeth less than half the length of the funnel-shaped corolla tube of the species *Jasminium fruticans*, I *experience* a jasmine flower with the rest of me. My brain can contribute nothing to the wonder of that experience, which is powerful and direct. God is in the experience. When I hear what my brain and a musical analyst tell me is 'a melody with a foreign chord which leads to G, the major submediant whose close leads to E flat, in which key, the subdominant, there is an interlude which drifts in dialogue into C flat (the flat supertonic)' the rest of me is transformed by the slow movement of Beethoven's Ninth Symphony. God is in the reality of that total experience.

And those other promptings in my past – the sudden impact of Wagner in Huddersfield Town Hall; of Leonardo's *Virgin of the Rocks* in the Louvre; of a mountain peak suddenly revealed as the mist clears; of John Donne's phrase 'O'er the white Alps alone'; of sensing the goodness in holy people; of suddenly catching a glimpse of my wife's face in a crowd; of those words from Father Amphilochios; and so many more – all these were experiences of God. These stabs of joy that make me love life so intensely, these are God. Not the God of the scholastics, whose existence I tried to discover intellectually for all those years, but the God of the child, before he becomes clever.

I experience God today in the loving kindness of people who acknowledge God as the sustainer of their being. To understand the experiences of joy I have I turn to such people. They have progressed further down the road than I ever shall, but I know that my journey is heading in the same, and for me the right, direction. The joy is the guarantor of that.

My faith is not an arbitrary and unverifiable assertion about an inaccessible reality. It is not a judgement which contradicts what I previously held to be true. It is simply a recognition of a reality which I have experienced. I do not see white now where previously I saw black: the difference is merely that my eyesight has improved. The reality which I perceive is not unimaginably distant but a direct personal experience which is its own authority. It is, I think, in this sense that Carl Jung, when asked on television whether he believed in God, replied, 'No. I do not believe. I know.'

I am at the beginning of a new road. I have chosen to take it after a long period of questioning and investigation because it seems to me the one most likely to lead to the truth, to an understanding of ultimate reality and to a fuller, richer life. I have not, I think, gone soft in the head. I still rely on my reason to do that which it does best – to discriminate between truth and error, between clear and muddled thinking when expressed in words. My reason has not proved to me the existence of God; combined with my experience, it has allowed me to accept his reality.

Petitionary prayer is still one of the mysteries of Christian life. When we ask for specific favours, which often involve suspension of or interference with natural law, what do we really expect to happen? One understanding I have reached is that miracles which happen after prayer must always have an alternative, rational, explanation, otherwise the recipient would lose free will. If God were to answer our prayers in an unambiguously miraculous way, the effect would be that we could no longer remain doubters. And it is only those who are free to deny who can freely believe. I suppose that miracles can, and do, happen to those who already firmly believe, since their free will is unaffected. But for most people they have to remain mysteries.

I have personal experience of one. I mentioned that, before her baptism into the Orthodox Church in early 1983, Felicia had been diagnosed by a consultant neurologist as suffering from multiple sclerosis. The symptoms – fierce headache and impaired vision and sensation – were intermittent but slowly worsened, and at the end of 1985 the priest of the Russian Orthodox Church in Exeter held a series of services for her recovery. I attended them, feeling slightly foolish as we stood in a circle with lighted candles and heard petitions for divine intervention that were a thousand years old.

After each service she felt much better, which I explained to myself was easily understandable as the psychological effect of being surrounded by affection, but the symptoms returned. After the series of services was completed, the symptoms seemed gradually to abate. In February 1986 she was examined by a consultant neurologist who pronounced her clear of multiple sclerosis and gave his opinion that she had never had it. So we were left with clear alternatives: original misdiagnosis, spontaneous remission, answered prayer. The mystery remains.

I had always accepted that people became religious because they could not tolerate uncertainty. They accepted things which were not true because they could not bear to go through their lives not knowing answers to the basic questions. Christianity gave answers to and provided the security for those who could not bear to live without them. Faith was popular because it brought the illusion of under-standing.

But I now *know* far fewer things than I did before I became a Christian. As a materialist, I knew that all life had emerged from a primeval sludge; that after death there was nothing; that the universe was heading nowhere in particular and that humanity had no destiny to fulfil but would quietly one day cease to exist as the sun cooled. Now I don't know these things any more. The extent of my ignorance has widened. I live with far more uncertainties than I did before I had faith. So Christianity is not a comforting illusion which provides answers but is the validation of mystery. And I can now acknowledge that the most important things in my life are those I don't now, and never will, understand.

A final note. During the war, as part of a campaign to save petrol, the Ministry of Information plastered posters all over England shouting the question IS YOUR JOURNEY REALLY NECESSARY? I think I would have to answer, in relation to the journey I have just described 'Not really.' Had I been more open to the truth, I should have found it without travelling. Only because I turned myself into such imperm-eable material did I have to journey so far to discover what had been available all along just down any road. Orthodoxy is neither Russian nor Greek. It is the inner essence of the original revelation of Christ, preserved in Russia and Greece against the rationalizing legalism of Western culture in general and the seemly reticence and moralizing of English

culture in particular. Orthodoxy can be found if you dig deep
enough into any of the mainstream Christian Churches.
Many English Christians know that and are happy with the
version of Christianity coloured by their own culture. I could
not see the essence for the colouring, and so went on a long
journey to find home.